Access to Justice for Business and Inclusive Growth in Latvia

OECD
BETTER POLICIES FOR BETTER LIVES

This work is published under the responsibility of the Secretary-General of the OECD. The opinions expressed and arguments employed herein do not necessarily reflect the official views of OECD member countries.

This document, as well as any data and any map included herein, are without prejudice to the status of or sovereignty over any territory, to the delimitation of international frontiers and boundaries and to the name of any territory, city or area.

Please cite this publication as:
OECD (2018), *Access to Justice for Business and Inclusive Growth in Latvia*, OECD Publishing, Paris.
https://doi.org/10.1787/9789264303416-en

ISBN 978-92-64-30340-9 (print)
ISBN 978-92-64-30341-6 (PDF)

The statistical data for Israel are supplied by and under the responsibility of the relevant Israeli authorities. The use of such data by the OECD is without prejudice to the status of the Golan Heights, East Jerusalem and Israeli settlements in the West Bank under the terms of international law.

Photo credits: Cover © Alex Tihonovs / Shutterstock.com.

Corrigenda to OECD publications may be found on line at: *www.oecd.org/about/publishing/corrigenda.htm*.

Foreword

As one of Europe's fastest-growing economies, Latvia recognises the importance of delivering effective legal and justice services to citizens and businesses to foster inclusive growth.

Despite the significant socio-economic challenges the country faced during the 2008-10 economic recession, Latvia made remarkable progress in the justice sector by implementing legal and structural reforms that create a climate that is conducive to doing business and building trust in public institutions. The country joins the trend among OECD countries of adopting a broader strategy to reinforce the justice system and public services based on user needs, thereby stimulating economic development and well-being. This trend entails more business-friendly administrations and lower administrative burdens. In pursuing administrative modernisation and simplification, Latvia is focused on making infrastructure responsive to business needs through more efficient and accessible public services and dispute resolution mechanisms.

Sustaining these efforts will be crucial to achieving Latvia's objectives in terms of sustainable development and economic growth.

Over the past twenty years, in an effort to strengthen the rule of law and the institutional foundations of economic development, policy makers and researchers alike have drawn considerable attention to the performance of the justice sector. Indeed, effective access to justice is increasingly seen as a key condition for creating a positive business and investment climate as well as a compelling means of tackling inequality. In this context, the OECD work on access to legal and justice services supports member and partner countries in designing and delivering responsive justice and legal services. This work also helps countries meet their commitments under the 2030 Agenda for Sustainable Development and implement the Inclusive Growth Agenda.

This report highlights not only the multiple strengths of Latvia's justice system, its legal and regulatory framework for commercial activities and service delivery for business, but also associated challenges. It provides recommendations to help the country realize its ambitions.

The report is also a testament to the Ministry of Justice's commendable consultation culture. During the consultations, stakeholders expressed their satisfaction with the openness of Latvian state institutions to consider their concerns. The assessment and recommendations presented here are based on a comprehensive review carried out by the OECD Secretariat as part of Latvia's accession process in 2014 as well as up-to-date information collected during fact-finding missions in June and October 2017. In addition, an online survey among businesses operating in Latvia was carried out in 2017. Final stakeholder consultations were conducted in March 2018 to validate the preliminary findings of this report.

We look forward to continue supporting Latvia on this path and to develop a truly accessible and effective justice system for Latvian citizens and businesses.

Marcos Bonturi
Director
OECD Public Governance Directorate

Acknowledgements

The OECD wishes to express its sincere gratitude for the generous financial and in-kind support of the Court Administration of the Republic of Latvia.

This report is part of the OECD work on Equal Access to Justice of the OECD Public Governance Directorate, under the direction of Marcos Bonturi. The work and report were led by Tatyana Teplova, Head of Unit, Governance for Gender and Inclusiveness, OECD Public Governance Directorate, under the guidance of Martin Forst, Head of Division, Governance Reviews and Partnerships, Daniel Trnka, Senior Policy Analyst and Nick Malyshev, Head of Division, Regulatory Policy Division. Principal authors of the report are Chloe Lelievre and Martyna Wanat, Policy Analysts, OECD Public Governance Directorate, Felix Steffek, University Lecturer, Faculty of Law; LLM Deputy Director; Deputy Director of the Centre for Corporate and Commercial Law; Director of Studies, Newnham College, University of Cambridge; Lorenzo Allio and Delia Rodrigo, Regulatory Reform Experts and Directors, allio|rodrigoconsulting.

Critical input was provided by Daniel Blume, OECD Directorate for Financial and Corporate Affairs.

The report was peer-reviewed and benefitted from further inputs provided by Tambet Artma, Head of Business Register Division and Kätlin Kattai, Head of Client and International Relations, Centre of Registers and Information Systems -RIK (Estonia); Bettina Meincke, Judge, Higher Regional Court of Cologne (Germany) and Farhaz Khan, Barrister, Outer Temple Chambers (United Kingdom).

The report also benefited from contributions by David Fauquié, lawyer, Barcelona (Spain).

A special appreciation is due to the governmental stakeholders including Deputy State Secretary of Justice Laila Medina, Edvīns Balševics, Anna Skrjabina and Lauma Legzdiņa from Court Administration, Baiba Lielkalne from the Ministry of Justice, Guna Paidere from the Enterprise Registry, the State Land Service, Land Registry offices, the Patent Office, the Ministry of Economy and the Ministry of Environmental Protection and Regional Development.

This report is the result of contributions from many businesses and other stakeholders who participated in the survey and interviews. The overall survey on access to business justice services was disseminated by the Court Administration and promoted through various governmental and business websites, including the Ministry of Economic, Investment and Development Agency of Latvia (LIAA), Enterprise Register, Patent Office; Latvian Chamber of Commerce and Industry and the Employers' Confederation of Latvia, Association of Latvian Commercial Banks, the Foreign Investors Council in Latvia (FICIL), the Latvian Start-up Association, Latvian Information and communications technology association (LIKTA), Certified Mediators Council and others. Interviews with business stakeholders during two fact-finding missions (July and October 2017), information received from Latvia and desk research also contributed to the findings of this report.

Sincere thanks are due to Jean-Jacques Hible, Paul Frissard, Dana Ghandour and Margaux Mery for their background research and inputs.

Editorial assistance was provided by Roxana Glavanov, Amelia Godber, Julie Harris and Andrew Esson. Administrative assistance was provided by Benjamin Jouannes and Charlotte Dubald.

Table of contents

Tables

Figures

Boxes

Executive summary

In July 2016, Latvia became OECD's 35th member country. It is one of the fastest-growing economies in Europe and offers an attractive business environment. While citizen satisfaction with public services in Latvia currently lies below the OECD average, trust in government and justice services has increased at a pace above the OECD average. This provides the momentum for taking stock and reflecting on opportunities to further strengthen access to justice so as to foster inclusive growth and a positive business climate.

A sound system of commercial legal and regulatory frameworks and well-functioning public services are important contributors to economic growth and social welfare. Commercial legislation and justice institutions support contracts and their enforcement, reduce transaction costs, and facilitate investment and trade. Effective access to justice for business also fosters good governance, legal certainty and predictability. This, in turn, enhances the development of entrepreneurship, an internationally attractive investment climate and private sector growth.

Like many OECD countries, Latvia is developing user-centred approaches to delivering legal and justice services to economic actors. The interests of different types of businesses serve as the guiding principle for evaluating legal and regulatory frameworks as well as related procedures. This report considers the perspective of a range of business types and sizes, individuals and specific groups.

The general institutional and legal framework plays a decisive role in creating a supportive business environment. Within this broader context, the following five issues currently stand out for Latvia: 1) a modern approach to commercial law; 2) formal requirements for doing business in the age of technology; 3) pace of reform and access to law; 4) strategies for reducing administrative burdens; 5) governance implications for business-friendly institutions.

These five issues are explored in more detail in the Assessment and recommendations.

Assessment and recommendations

A modern approach to the Commercial Law

Latvia's "Commercial Law" serves as the basis for creating, managing and closing businesses. The business stakeholders consulted for this report expressed general satisfaction with the provisions of this law and its implementation. The stakeholders are also generally satisfied with the services provided by the state bodies involved, namely the Enterprise Registry, the State Land Service and Land Registry offices and the Patent Office. Nonetheless, two issues for improvement were identified. First, courts and public services were at times seen to take an unnecessarily strict approach in applying the Commercial Law. For example, when a matter is not regulated in the Commercial Law, state institutions often assume that it is prohibited rather than providing the parties with the freedom to contract. Second, entrepreneurs identified the need to adapt the Commercial Law to modern forms of business and finance, such as start-ups and crowdfunding.

Formal requirements for doing business in the age of technology

Latvia's Digital Agenda and e-Government Strategy are powerful drivers of administrative simplification. While there are important initiatives to further develop and mainstream information and communication technology in the public administration, many e-government initiatives are managed by different actors targeting various stakeholders, and often appear to be disconnected from each other.

Many stakeholders suggested reducing the formal requirements in their interaction with the Enterprise Registry. Notably, they proposed a reduction or even abolition of many requirements to provide documents in notarised form. Other stakeholders suggested modernising such requirements instead. Taking into account developments in other OECD countries, the reduction of formal requirements and the introduction of electronic solutions may help reduce costs and create benefits for business.

Pace of reform and access to law

Like other countries, Latvia faces the challenge of balancing a timely reaction to reform needs with a need for legal certainty and predictability. Entrepreneurs, public services and courts seem to agree that the Latvian legal system is developing in the right direction. At the same time, all of them find the hectic rhythm of legal reform difficult to follow. Empirical research found in 2016 that the biggest obstacle to business growth was "frequent changes in laws and regulations" (identified by 66% of participants). Similarly, stakeholders felt that the Commercial Law and procedural rules are not always accessible. Foreign investors find that Latvian laws and some relevant websites are not consistently available in an up-to-date English version.

Shaping a business-friendly governance

Latvia is well on its way to establishing organisational and procedural governance that fosters business-friendly state institutions, not least by seeking to match the top world performers in terms of facilitating business and stimulating entrepreneurship. Reformers in the public administration enjoy a high level of credibility and trust with stakeholders. Currently, however, there is no document that sets out the government-wide vision for integrating access to justice and inclusive growth in regulatory policy. Informal agreements between ministries seem to replace more formal co-ordination.

One of the most visible and successful measures of the government's programme to make administration more user-friendly is the "Consult First" project. This project, explicitly based on OECD guidance, advises businesses before sanctioning them. Legal rules that are considered essential, however, may still be enforced without prior advice.

Centring state and dispute resolution services on business needs

During the course of their activities, small, medium-sized and large businesses engage with various public services in numerous ways. They register their existence and activities, apply for licences, file their accounts and tax documentation, try to solve their disputes and so on. Small and medium-sized enterprises sometimes lack capabilities and resources for such activities. The OECD Serving Citizens Framework emphasises that public services, courts and alternative dispute resolution mechanisms should reflect the interests and needs of users, be they businesses or citizens. Consequently, Latvia carried out a survey to establish the needs and experiences of businesses when accessing services under the purview of the Ministry of Justice.

Strategies for reducing administrative burdens

Latvia is continually working to simplify the statutory and administrative framework. Stakeholders and state institutions engage in a sustained dialogue to identify measures for improvement. Representatives of both the private sector and public bodies value this approach. Despite many efforts under way, Latvia has not yet carried out a larger programme to measure the statutory and administrative burdens of existing institutions and regulations, for instance by applying quantitative methodologies such as the Standard Cost Model. Simplification programmes appear to be based on qualitative assessments and perception surveys. This report, for example, applies the Standard Cost Model to three commercial procedures: the registration of an individual merchant, the registration of a limited liability company and the reorganisation of a company through a merger by acquisition.

A continuum of public services for businesses

"One-stop shops" are services that are bundled at one central access point. They are recognised throughout the OECD as efficient and comprehensive entry points to public administration. However, one-stop shops are often a challenge to put into practice. In Latvia, the Public Administration Services Portal (www.latvija.lv), managed by the State Regional Development Agency, provides access to a growing number of e-services. In addition, the Ministry of Economy launched an initiative to create a one-stop-shop website for businesses. Stakeholders have mentioned uncoordinated and multiple requests for information by public administrative bodies, which can lead to incoherent decisions and unpredictability.

The provision of e-services is necessary to streamline administrative procedures for businesses. Information technology is used both at the front end presented to users and the back end dealing with data management and decision making. The Latvian government is actively engaged in securing the circulation of data among state institutions as well as the provision of e-services to end users. This process seems to be in a transitional stage. Important decisions were made, but further fundamental steps need to be taken. The electronic identification of citizens and businesses remains fragmented and not easily accessible. Stakeholders reported some progress, but noted that they could not fully access electronic services regardless of location. While entrepreneurs are increasingly aware of e-signature services, they are not making full use of them. With regard to the back end, Latvia would benefit from establishing integrated data management covering all public services. A common data protocol and common data standards for all public services are also key to the one-stop-shop approach, although these can be difficult to achieve in practice.

Business-related services under the Ministry of Justice

Commercial registries facilitate commercial organisation and transactions. They document rights, act as gatekeepers and provide information. Registries in Latvia include the Enterprise Registry, the State Land Service and Land Registry offices as well as the Patent Office. Stakeholders are generally satisfied with the services offered and trust the Enterprise Registry. Surveyed stakeholders mention the simplification and minimisation of data requirements as a primary issue for improvement. Efforts in this direction are already under way. Stakeholder comments indicate that the number of inactive companies on the register is high, raising legitimacy issues as to their purpose. The Standard Cost Model analysis conducted as part of this project reveals the high importance users give to waiting time for registering entries. Greater use of e-service solutions can speed up procedures. While the use of e-platform services grew from 38% in 2014 to 42% in 2016, further efforts are needed

Stakeholders are generally happy with the services provided by the State Land Service and Land Registry offices, although the separation of the cadastre and register functions into two entities is often seen as limiting efficiency, data consistency and accessibility. Currently, only a few businesses apply online for registration services.

The Patent Office is the central authority of the Latvian industrial property protection system. Most respondents surveyed were satisfied, if not very satisfied, with the service provided. The experience of the Patent Office shows the advantages of e-platform services over e-signature services in terms of cost savings.

A continuum of dispute resolution services

OECD countries are increasingly promoting a wide range of legal and justice services, recognising that disputes can be effectively and efficiently resolved through various pathways. These pathways to justice are part of a continuum of services ranging from alternative dispute resolution (mediation, conciliation, ombudschemes, arbitration) to contentious litigation in court. The inability to solve legal conflicts may have a negative effect on businesses and society. Businesses may suffer financial costs (e.g. loss of income), social costs (e.g. damaged employee relations) and reputational costs (e.g.

damage to business relationships), and – in extreme cases – businesses may cease trading. Indeed 59% and 54% of 37 surveyed businesses stated that the barriers to access to justice for businesses are time and costs, respectively.

Access to a sound court system is an essential element of a good dispute resolution framework. Latvia extensively reformed its court system to establish a clear three-level instance structure. A recent reform also decreased the duration of proceedings: from 9.2 months in 2013 to 7.4 in 2017 for civil cases, from 6.4 months in 2013 to 5.4 in 2017 for criminal cases, and from 13.5 months in 2013 to 7.5 in 2017 for administrative cases. Like several OECD countries, Latvia is integrating e-services, such as electronic case management, into its court system to address the barriers to justice (duration, cost and complexity).

Another relevant issue emphasised by stakeholders concerns specialised court proceedings. Latvia currently makes limited use of specialisation. While there is no comprehensive specialisation policy, some specialised tracks have been introduced. For example, the court at Jelgava hears cases concerning shareholder resolutions. Different degrees of specialisation are possible: specialised courts, specialised chambers or informal specialised tracks. While there are possible drawbacks (for example, compartmentalisation of the knowledge of judges and preferential treatment of repeat users) and cost considerations, the potential advantages of specialisation are efficiency and effectiveness in the resolution of questions of law, enhanced uniformity and predictability as well as improved quality of judicial decision making.

Access to effective alternative dispute resolution (ADR) can be as important as access to courts. The challenge for lawmakers is to design a justice system that supports parties in bringing their dispute to the right forum, depending on its nature and severity. While there is considerable interest in ADR in Latvia, it is not adequately used in practice. Conflict parties do not really consider the full spectrum of dispute resolution mechanisms and there are gaps in the ADR services on offer. Businesses only rarely seem to contemplate arbitration, mediation, conciliation, ombudschemes or online dispute resolution. Like many other countries, Latvia grapples with the low practical relevance of mediation despite its attractive characteristics. In arbitration, the supply of and demand for services are currently not balanced. Conciliation and ombudschemes are much less established than in other OECD countries.

Recommendations

Responding to business needs: A favourable framework for doing business in Latvia

A modern approach to the Commercial Law

Recommendation 1: Legislative amendments could help clarifying the interpretation of the Commercial Law where needed. Courts and public services could also contribute to an enabling culture through a more facilitative interpretation of the Commercial Law.

Recommendation 2: The scope of the Latvian Commercial Law could be expanded to include modern forms of business organisation and their financing. This should not be understood as a call for new hard laws, but rather a systematic regulatory approach taking into account all types of regulation, ranging from soft law and self-regulation to mandatory law.

Formal requirements for doing business in the age of technology

Recommendation 3: A more centralised, integrated approach to adopting technology could help improve efficiency. Making sure that all public services take part in this initiative and are bound by the government agenda will increase the benefits for business.

Recommendation 4: Consider reducing the formal requirements in the Commercial Law along with introducing electronic forms of documents and identification.

Pace of reform and access to law

Recommendation 5: Reform amendments could be enacted as packages in less frequent waves. Reform initiatives could be explained to the public by concentrating on key measures and principles. Websites and other information should be better structured, for example, by structurally reflecting the events in the life of a business (such as creation, paying taxes and liquidation). Laws and relevant websites could also be made available in English.

Shaping a business-friendly governance

Recommendation 6: Consider developing a single, formal, whole-of-government document setting out the regulatory policy of the government. It might also be worth considering developing systematic *ex post* reviews of existing regulations as part of a development planning system and fostering public sector skills to use analytical tools.

Recommendation 7: A formal, comprehensive policy co-ordinating the activities of all ministries in the realm of businesses would make the Latvian better regulation agenda more effective. This policy should also assign responsibilities and milestones to be achieved to ensure accountability within the government and to the public.

Recommendation 8: As part of the "Consult First" initiative, it would be important to clarify which rules are essential and which are not. Stakeholders also suggested establishing the "Consult First" initiative as a right for businesses as opposed to a discretionary solution for the relevant state agency.

Strategies for reducing administrative burdens

Recommendation 9: Establishing inter-institutional working groups to review existing laws and public services is good practice. A further emphasis on evidence-based and quantitative research methodologies will help to avoid the pitfalls of using anecdotal evidence as a basis for legal reform. The Standard Cost Model, as applied in this report, provides an idea of the utility of empirical and quantitative methods for law making.

Centring state and dispute resolution services on business needs

A continuum of public services for businesses

Recommendation 10: Latvia should consider developing a model of legal and justice services to capture the legal needs of businesses and other users, and to understand their pathways and experience as well as the gaps in the provision of services. Consider two interrelated approaches: institution-generated or "administrative" data and legal needs surveys.

Recommendation 11: Latvian public services that could be part of a one-stop-shop approach include the Enterprise Registry, the State Land Service, Land Registry offices, the Patent Office, the Tax Authority and relevant licencing authorities. These could also include legal assistance services and referrals to various dispute resolution mechanisms. Ideally, businesses should not have to differentiate between the competences of state agencies or have to identify with the relevant legal provisions. In addition, users should only be required to provide a certain piece of information once.

Recommendation 12: Latvia could consider creating a service delivery model that includes the intersection between the digital and physical realms (e.g. using video communication) as well as ensure broad coverage of fast optical fibre cable based internet across the territory.

Recommendation 13: The user-centred one-stop-shop approach should establish common data management covering all public services, including common data protocol and common data standards and interfaces. One way to improve the communication between users and agencies is the publication of easy-to-use and easy-to-access best practice guidelines. Such guidelines can create a common ground between agencies and users and will improve the acceptance of procedures and results.

Recommendation 14: The government could consider steps to increase the uptake of e-services through a mandatory e-signature. An e-residency approach might be helpful, in particular to improve investment opportunities for foreigners. Ultimately, e-platform solutions offer more attractive cost-benefit outcomes than mere e-signature solutions. Central data management would be a first and important step towards a more coherent decision making process. Establishing an institutional and procedural framework that ensures full participation of all service providers is key.

Business-related services under the Ministry of Justice

Recommendation 15: The Enterprise Registry and other public services under the Ministry of Justice should provide more and better online information. Optimising the data exchange among business services and integrating licencing services would foster business development in Latvia. This approach, coupled with e-service solutions, would further decrease waiting time. A combination of mixed measures (filing duties, penalties and the threat to strike entities off the register) could be used to distinguish legitimate inactive companies from illegitimate ones.

Recommendation 16: Evaluate the challenges and solutions with regard to the separation of cadastre and land register functions into two administrative entities. Some countries group both services in one institution, others use technology to solve efficiency, data consistency and user accessibility problems. Implementing e-services and encouraging stakeholders to use electronic registration in land transactions could lead to cost savings and pave the way for a one-stop-shop service structure.

A continuum of dispute resolution services

Recommendation 17: Latvia may benefit from adopting a more user-centric approach and develop a policy for a continuum of dispute resolution services including their integration into one-stop-shops. This would go hand-in-hand with increasing the use of information technology in the court system.

Recommendation 18: Develop and implement a comprehensive strategy for alternative dispute resolution (ADR). This concerns all facets of ADR, for example mediation, conciliation, ombudschemes and arbitration. Raising business awareness about mediation should be coupled with strengthening the capacity of service providers. An evaluation could reveal whether further action on mediation is needed by the legislature or other standard-setting bodies. Thought should be given to make ombudschemes and conciliation more relevant to business stakeholders.

Recommendation 19: Continue to reduce the time and cost of services in relation to capacity needs including at the prevention stage e.g. providing information. Better assess the financial burden of court services for business' opportunity costs (e.g. time off work or transportation due to geographic isolation).

Recommendation 20: Develop a comprehensive strategy towards specialisation including updating the training needs of judges and staff. Like other countries, Latvia might also consider introducing English as an optional language for certain types of court proceedings.

Chapter 1. Overview of the legal system and governance in Latvia

This chapter provides an overview of the current situation in Latvia and its legal system and governance structure. It focuses on the socio-economic context and examines determinants for a sound business and investment climate. Latvia's performance is demonstrated based on international benchmarks. This chapter highlights the importance of a sound legal system and effective well-functioning of justice for long-term economic and social outcomes and a thriving business environment.

Governance background

Following its independence in 1991 and the dissolution of the Soviet Union, Latvia underwent important political, economic and structural changes as it transitioned into a small democratic country with a market-based economy. Latvia became the 35th OECD member country in July 2016; it joined the European Union in 2004 and has had access to the Schengen area since 2007 and the Eurozone since 2014.

Latvia is a multiparty parliamentary republic, divided into 119 administrative entities, including 110 municipalities and 9 cities. The president is the head of state elected by the *Saeima* (parliament) with the prime minister politically responsible for the fulfilment of presidential duties under the constitution. Legislative authority is vested in the *Saeima*, a unicameral parliament comprised of 100 deputies that are elected by proportional representation for four-year terms.

The Judiciary is led by the Supreme Court. The Latvian court system consists of three levels of courts and the Prosecutor's Office. Ordinary courts or courts of general jurisdiction deal with civil and criminal matters and a specialised jurisdiction hears administrative cases. The Constitutional Court functions separately from the three-tiered court system.

The overall budgetary situation of Latvia is strong; government finances remain solid with low public debt. Latvia benefits from different European financial instruments (e.g. European Structural and Investment Funds, ESIF) boosting investment (OECD, 2017a).

Trust in government, including justice, is generally low compared to OECD countries (Figure 1.1). But it has been increasing since 2007, at a pace above the OECD average.

Figure 1.1. Confidence in national government in 2016 and its change since 2017

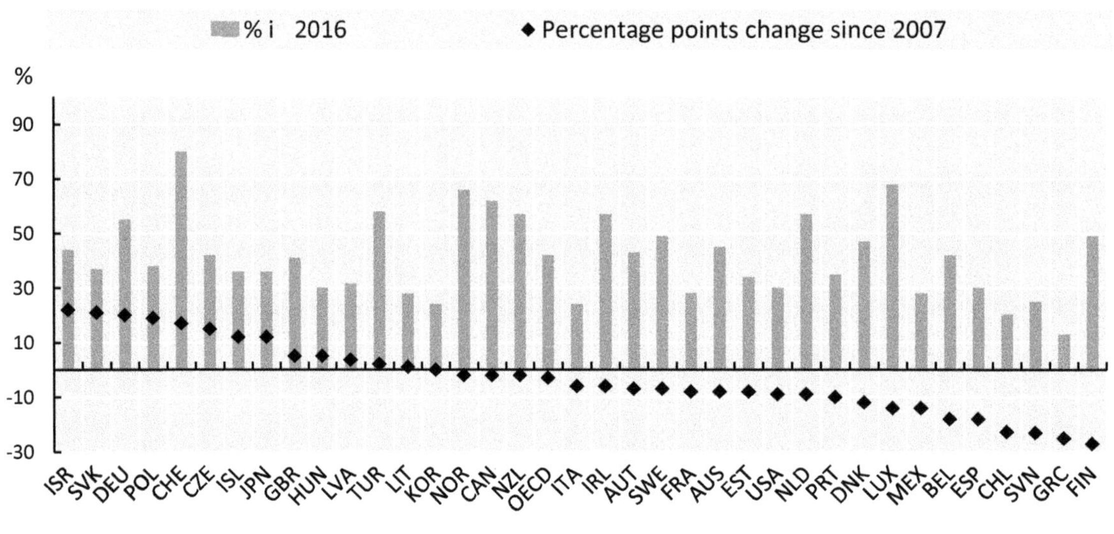

Source: Adapted from Gallup World Poll in OECD (2017b).

Citizen satisfaction and confidence levels with public services also remain below the OECD average (Figure 1.2). With regards to the judicial system, Latvians cite low legal awareness, limited objectivity in the treatment of citizens, unequal access to public services and timeliness of the court system as the main issues. Nonetheless, due to a broad range of reform initiatives introduced by the government, trust in the judicial system has increased since 2014, from 31% to 41% in 2016 (OECD, 2017c, 2015a).

Figure 1.2. Citizen satisfaction and confidence in public services, 2016

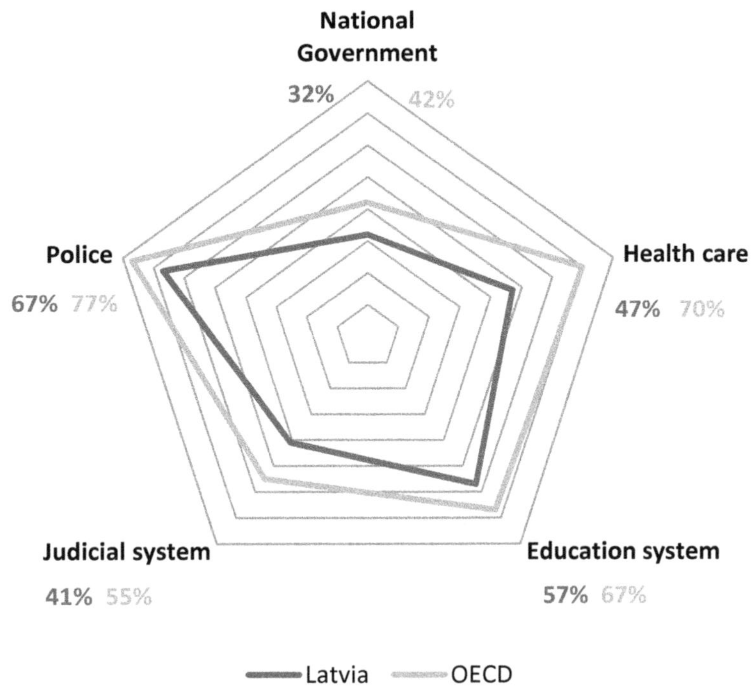

Source: Adapted from OECD (2017c).

The socio-economic context for a sound business and investment climate

In recent years, Latvia's economy has become one of the fastest-growing economies in Europe (OECD, 2017d) with a positive business environment (EBRD, 2016). Latvia rapidly and consistently recovered from the 2008 global crisis and its 2007-10 recession. In 2016, its economic growth slowed down but picked up during 2017 (Figure 1.3). Latvia's economic dynamism builds on stronger domestic demand and its open approach to global trade and investment (OECD, 2017a). It is exposed to international developments and its main trading partners, Estonia, Germany, Lithuania Poland and the Russian Federation, with links to other CIS (Commonwealth of Independent States) economies. There exist regional disparities, particularly in the eastern and rural regions: the Riga metropolitan area is a key driver of economic growth, contributing about 69% to the national gross domestic product (GDP) (OECD, 2017e). Informal activity is widespread – estimated at more than 20% of GDP in 2015 (OECD, 2017a).

Figure 1.3. Economic growth in Latvia, 2010-17

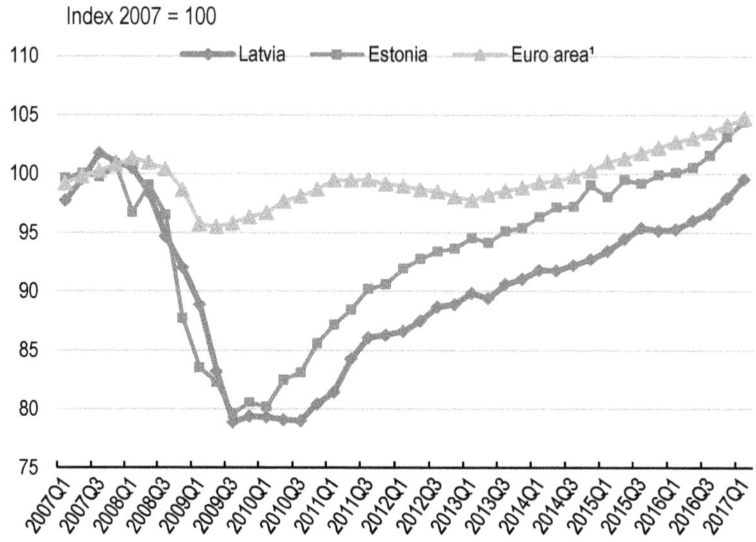

1. Euro area countries which are OECD members.
2. Percentage gap with respect to the weighted average using population weights of the highest 17 OECD countries in terms of GDP per capita and GDP per hour worked (in constant 2010 PPPs).
Source: OECD (2017f); OECD (2017g); OECD (2017h).

Latvia recently implemented numerous legal and structural reforms in labour market, tax and business among others (OECD, 2017i). These reforms are stimulating growth and well-being (OECD, 2017h). It considered the most structural reform priorities identified in the "OECD Going for Growth" initiative, compared to other OECD countries (OECD, 2017e). The Latvian government adopted a number of legislative and procedural changes in order to bring national legislation into conformity with the international standards of the OECD, the European Union, and the World Trade Organization. Regulations regarding the creation of new businesses (including the associated time and costs) and operation of private enterprises appear easy and not burdensome. According to the latest World Bank Doing Business Report, Latvia is ranked 19th out of 190 countries in terms of ease of doing business (Figure 1.4)[1]. It is the 21st economy worldwide in terms of starting a business, keeping pace with its neighbouring countries and ranking above the average score of OECD countries (Box 1.1).

Figure 1.4. Starting a Business in Latvia and comparable economies

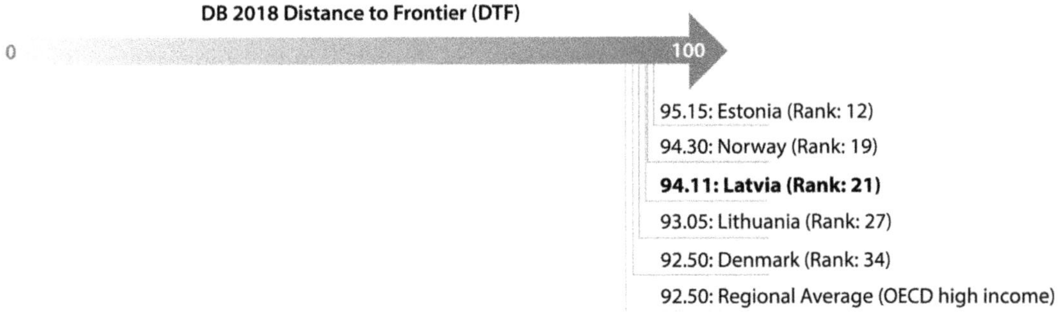

Note: The distance to frontier (DTF) measure shows the distance of each economy to the "frontier," which represents the best performance observed on each of the indicators across all economies in the Doing Business sample since 2005. An economy's distance to frontier is reflected on a scale from 0 to 100, where 0 represents the lowest performance and 100 represents the frontier. The ease of doing business ranking ranges from 1 to 190.
Source: Adapted from World Bank (2018).

Box 1.1. Latvia's business environment: An international benchmark

While steady reforms have improved Latvia's ranking in the World Bank Doing Business Index over the years, the Doing Business 2018 profile records a worsening of the country's overall score compared to the previous year. Latvia ranks 19th among the 190 world economies considered, moving down five places. In 2018, Latvia follows its regional partners – Denmark (3rd), Norway (8th), Estonia (12th) and Lithuania (16th) – but remains above the OECD average. The "Starting a business" indicator remains stable compared to 2017.

With regard to the Global Competitiveness Index (GCI), Latvia ranks 49th overall among 140 countries in 2016-17 (previously 44th place), while in the execution of essential requirements (institutional environment, quality of public infrastructure, macroeconomic environment, health and primary education) Latvia moved down from 37th to 41st place.

With regards to strengthening effectiveness (higher education, goods market and labour market efficiency, financial market development, technological readiness, and market size), Latvia moved down from 39th to 42nd place. The index of business satisfaction and innovation remained unchanged in 2016-17 compared to the previous year, stabilising Latvia at 58th place.

In comparison to the other Baltic countries Estonia (30th place) and Lithuania (35th place), the Latvian Ministry of Economy identifies Latvia's weaknesses as being in infrastructure, macroeconomic environment, healthcare, higher education, financial market development, business sophistication, innovations and technological readiness.

Source: World Bank (2018); World Economic Forum (2016); Latvian Ministry of Economy (2017).

In addition, due diligence principles of corporate social responsibility (CSR)/responsible business conduct are widely promoted by the Ministry of Welfare, the Employers' Confederation of Latvia and the American Chamber of Commerce in Latvia (Box 1.2). Latvia's framework for corporate governance is found largely consistent with the G20/OECD Principles of Corporate Governance, and it appears to broadly protect and facilitate the exercise of rights (OECD, 2017d).

Box 1.2. Microindex and the Sustainability Index

The Latvian National Contact Point, together with the Employers' Confederation of Latvia and the Latvia Free Trade Union, launched the "Microindex", an evaluation methodology for small and medium-sized enterprises (SMEs) and micro-enterprises that aims to further sustainable development and corporate social responsibility (CSR) best practices. The index provides SMEs and their suppliers with the opportunity to objectively review their work and evaluate the need for improvements. It examines five spheres of enterprise activity: long-term business strategy, work environment, market relations, environment, and community. Participating companies publish the results of 40 criteria online at www.ilgtspeja.lv/atbildigabiznesanovertejums.

The "Microindex" is incorporated in Latvia's annual "Sustainability Index", an initiative that assists companies to develop, implement and measure their sustainable practice and encourages companies to integrate corporate responsibility into their business strategy. It also sets objective criteria for the community and public and non-governmental organisations to evaluate and support companies contributing to the long-term sustainability of the Latvian economy, environment, and society. The methodology used in both indices was developed by a wide range of Latvian experts based on global examples such as the Dow Jones Sustainability Index and Corporate Responsibility (CR) Index by Business in the Community, and is in alignment with ISO 26000 and the Global Reporting Initiative guidelines. The results are published at www.ilgtspejasindekss.lv.

Source: Extracted from OECD (2014a).

As in other Baltic States, the capital market in Latvia is small. The most competitive sectors are woodworking, metalworking, transportation, information technology (IT), green tech, healthcare, life science, food processing and finance; some of which were identified by the Latvian Investment and Development Agency as having the highest potential for new investment (US Department of State, 2017). State-owned enterprises (SOEs) represent a great part of the market (OECD, 2017d); however, "private enterprises may compete with SOEs on the same terms and conditions" (US Department of State, 2017). A levelled playing field is one of the core corporate governance principles in Latvia. The outright majority of enterprises operating in Latvia are micro, small and medium-sized companies (OECD, 2017d).

As mentioned above, Latvia's economy is also strongly driven by trade; the value of exports and imports equals 119% of GDP (Heritage Foundation, 2017). Latvian export products and markets have diversified and improved, however, Latvia still largely relies on raw materials and natural-resource-intensive products (OECD, 2017e). Latvia's three largest export markets are Lithuania, Estonia and the Russian Federation (OECD, 2017e). Participation in global value chains continues to be low; few successful Latvian firms have much higher productivity, employment and wages in comparison to overall entrepreneurship in the country (OECD, 2017e). In addition, skills mismatch and widespread informality prevent firms from entering global value chains (OECD, 2017e).

Unemployment in Latvia decreased recently, yet remains high (OECD, 2017a). The official rate of registered unemployment is above 8%, with a high proportion between the ages15-24 (OECD, 2017e). There is a high incidence of long-term unemployment, adding to widespread poverty. And the high unemployment rate likely reflects regional and skills mismatches between workers and jobs (OECD, 2017a).

Significant skills shortage and mismatch are factors that have held back productivity in Latvia for many years (OECD, 2017g, 2016b). For instance, in 2013 a third of employers mentioned an inadequately educated workforce as a constraint on their activities and the business environment more generally (EBRD, 2016). It significantly impedes adoption of advanced technologies and management practices (OECD, 2017e). There is a need to provide more training for the unemployed with better income support; it could help tackle unemployment, provide qualified employees matching economic needs and widely distribute benefits of economic growth (OECD, 2017a).

Introducing policies to enhance the participation of women in the labour force and to access well-paid positions could further improve the supply of skills (OECD, 2017e). Women constitute 55% of the labour market in Latvia (OECD, 2016c). The share of women in civil service is 63.7% while 54% are in senior positions (OECD, 2017c). The female share of seats on boards of the largest publicly listed companies amounts to 28% (OECD, 2016d).

According to the OECD's Better Life Index, Latvians are less satisfied with their lives than the OECD average (Figure 1.5). The most impaired dimensions highlighted by the Better Life Index are: access to well-paid jobs, the healthcare system and housing. In addition to long-run unemployment, weak social safety nets and high taxes on low wage incomes contribute to informality, low poverty and the emigration of young people. Additional public spending is required to improve economic opportunities, access to housing, healthcare and education.

Figure 1.5. Well-being in Latvia

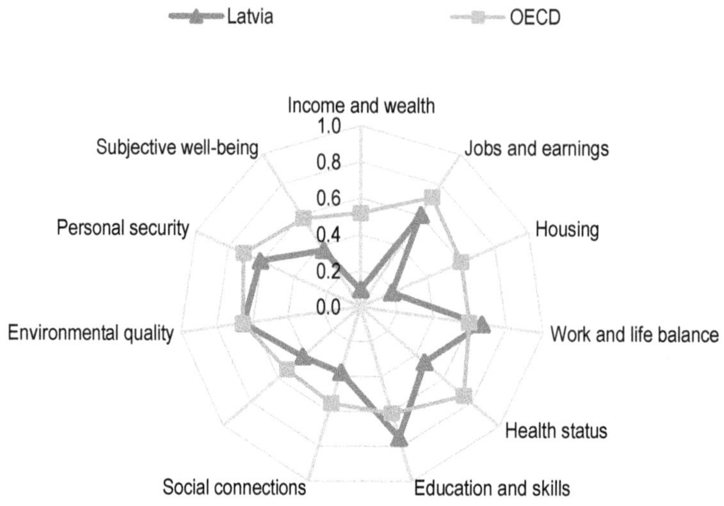

Source: OECD (2017e).

Law and access to justice for doing business and inclusive growth

A sound legal system and the effective functioning of justice institutions are key contributors to long-term economic and social outcomes and a thriving business environment (OECD, 2013; Acemoglu, Johnson and Robinson, 2005). The rule of law, justice and access to redress may support contract enforcement, reduce transaction costs (which are impeded by theft, corruption, weak property rights, etc.) and facilitate longer-term investments and engagement in trade for stakeholders (Acemoglu, Johnson and Robinson, 2005).

A sound and clear legal framework supports steady economic growth by creating an enabling business environment and strengthening the national marketplace in which economic activity takes place (OECD, 2015c). Moreover, it contributes to the attractiveness of the national legal system in the global marketplace, in particular with regard to business activities (OECD, 2010a). Maintaining such a legal framework feeds into the economic and social well-being of citizens, distributing the benefits across society. A legitimate and equally accessible judicial system is found to maintain business markets by determining "the rules of the game", securing fair competition and protecting property rights. It is also an essential factor for fostering good governance, legal certainty and predictability, thereby enhancing the development of business and investment climates and supporting private sector growth in compliance with outlined regulatory frameworks (OECD, 2015d).

Strengthening access to justice is thus necessary to create a supportive environment for business and to enable a level playing field for economic stakeholders, including SMEs. The OECD Policy Framework for Investment (PFI) suggests that when key elements of effective access to justice are missing or inefficient (e.g. complex, costly, and lengthy procedures), companies including SMEs may limit their activities (OECD, 2015c). Perceived ability to settle a potential dispute efficiently and effectively, including enforcing a contract and securing property rights can unlock investment decisions. The rule of law, including effective, timely and efficient justice and legal services can give businesses the chance to thrive, taking into consideration elements such as the level of impact on regulatory frameworks, addressing skills mismatch, R&D, access to finance, more equitable financial markets that channel resources into productive activities, and any accompanying restructuring and displacement.

Addressing the legal needs of businesses: A driver for growth

Building on the strong tradition of legal needs surveys of individual citizens, OECD countries are increasingly focusing on understanding the legal needs of business in order to improve the business environment and promote socio-economic growth. The traditional approach to the delivery of legal and justice services mainly focused on institutional performance. It does not consider the types of justice problems businesses have, what institutions they engage, the "effectiveness" of legal dispute mechanisms and what works, for whom and for what types of legal and justice needs.

This report places particular emphasis on addressing the legal needs of businesses as a driver for inclusive growth. There is growing evidence that the ability to address legal problems can contribute to inclusive growth by creating jobs, reducing work days missed due to legal problems, providing stable housing, resolving debt issues and stimulating business activities.

The shift towards user centricity (e.g. needs of different types of business) serves as the guiding principle to design the policy agenda and evaluate legal and justice service content and delivery. It considers the perspective of a range of business types and sizes, individuals and specific groups, and aims to inform the design of services that are more responsive to business needs. This is expected to be translated into achieving efficiency and the sound functioning of the justice system.

Balancing user perspectives with public interest

Importantly, Latvia recognises the importance of a robust system of legal and justice services in addressing market-related challenges, such as: corruption, insider trading and abusive self-dealing. The efficiency of the judiciary was enhanced by the consolidation of small district courts. Nonetheless, as mentioned, trust in the justice system remains a challenge, similar to other public institutions (OECD, 2017c).

OECD work confirms that the effectiveness of justice systems and the sound commercial law framework have an important role in stimulating competitiveness and economic development (OECD, 2016e, 2014b). It is recognised that it is dependent, among other things, "on the existence and fulfilment of clear laws and norms, most importantly the legal certainty of firms and contracts guaranteed by trustworthy and objective court systems […] the idea being that regions that lack such legal systems impose higher transaction costs to market participants" (OECD/IMCO, 2013). The security of property rights, justice institutions, contract and debt enforcement, and mortgage contracts are of great relevance.

Objectives and organisation of this report

Improving access to justice is increasingly recognised as a critical dimension of inclusive growth and as a means of improving citizen well-being and economic performance (OECD, 2015e). In this context, countries are developing user-centred approaches to delivering legal and justice services (OECD, 2015f). Latvia joins this global trend, adopting a broader strategy to strengthen not just the judicial sector, but also law enforcement authorities. An overall assessment of the justice sector serves to encourage evidence-based policies that deliver swift, reliable and trustworthy justice.

Given that Latvia started implementing extensive measures to reflect the needs of businesses, the OECD was invited to undertake a mapping of legal needs and review the accessibility and responsiveness of governmental justice services (i.e. Enterprise Registry; Patent Office, State Land Service and Land Registry offices; Courts and Alternative Dispute Resolution mechanisms). Building on these needs and the experience of businesses, the assessment further aims to identify the crucial problems for businesses in the implementation of the Commercial Law and regulatory framework and their suitability to the different forms of commercial activity.

This report draws from the comprehensive review carried out by the OECD Secretariat as part of Latvia's accession process in 2014, as well as from direct insights and up-to-date information collected during fact-finding missions to Riga and strategy meetings, which took place in March, June, August and October 2017. In addition, OECD undertook an online survey among business stakeholders operating in Latvia (with around 300 respondents). The data results should be interpreted with caution, however, and should be considered jointly with the results of stakeholder interviews and consultations. The survey was disseminated by the Court Administration and promoted through various governmental and business websites. Wide stakeholder consultation was conducted in March 2018 focusing on the substantive issues and to validate the preliminary findings of the first draft report.

Chapter 1 presents and discusses the current organisational and procedural arrangements deployed by the government to pursue administrative simplification and promote an increasingly business-friendly environment in Latvia. By placing specific focus on procedures regulated by the Latvian Commercial Law, the chapter seeks to identify actions that could further facilitate doing business based on evidence drawn from Chapter 3 related to costs associated with administrative procedures.

Chapter 2 examines the accessibility of services for businesses and presents a concept of a continuum of legal and justice services. In line with the OECD Serving Citizen framework it focuses on services provided by the state (Enterprise Registry, State Land service and Registry and the Patent Office). The chapter places a particular emphasis on digital tools and provides an overview of e-services available for businesses in Latvia. This chapter also identifies the characteristics and impact of legal problems experienced by Latvian businesses.

Chapter 3 seeks to measure administrative costs related to selected procedures prescribed under the Commercial Law. It identifies and analyses possible simplification measures that may support the starting-up or re-organisation of business operations and translate into cost savings. The main focus of this chapter is on reducing the administrative burden generated from selected business registration procedures administered by the Latvian Enterprise Registry i.e., registrations of an individual merchant and a limited liability company with decreased capital, and reorganisation of a limited liability company through merger by acquisition. The chapter presents evidence that may substantiate legal amendments and changes in procedural practice presented in Chapter 1, and make the relationship with businesses more efficient.

Note

[1] We note, on the other hand, that the World Bank Doing Business Index also stops its "starting a business" procedure at the moment the registration at the State Revenue Service ends. Businesses in Latvia must still comply with additional procedures before starting their activities.

References

Acemoglu, D., S. Johnson and J.A. Robinson (2005), Institutions as a Fundamental Cause of Long-Run Growth, , Handbook of Economic Growth, Vol. 1A, Chapter 6, Elsevier B.V., pp. 385–472, DOI: 001: lO.l016/Sl574-W84(05)OloW-3.

EBRD (European Bank for Reconstruction and Development) (2016), "Strategy for Latvia", as approved by the Board of Directors at its meeting on 10 February 2016.

Heritage Foundation (2017), *2017 Index of Economic Freedom,* www.heritage.org/index/pdf/2017/book/index_2017.pdf (accessed 30 January 2018).

Latvia - Ministry of Economy (2017), "Action Plan for Improvement of the Business Environment".

OECD (2017a), "Latvia", in *OECD Economic Outlook, Volume 2017 Issue 2*, OECD Publishing, Paris, http://dx.doi.org/10.1787/eco_outlook-v2017-2-31-en.

OECD (2017b), *Government at a Glance 2017*, OECD Publishing, Paris, *http://dx.doi.org/10.1787/gov_glance-2017-en*

OECD (2017c), *Government at a Glance 2017, Country Fact Sheet, Latvia*, www.oecd.org/gov/gov-at-a-glance-2017-latvia.pdf.

OECD (2017d), *Corporate Governance in Latvia*, OECD Publishing, Paris, http://dx.doi.org/10.1787/9789264268180-en.

OECD (2017e), *OECD Economic Surveys: Latvia 2017*, OECD Publishing, Paris, http://dx.doi.org/10.1787/eco_surveys-lva-2017-en.

OECD (2017f), *OECD Economic Outlook: Statistics and Projections* (database), http://dx.doi.org/10.1787/eo-data-en.

OECD (2017g), *OECD National Accounts Statistics* (database), http://dx.doi.org/10.1787/na-data-en.

OECD (2017h), *OECD Productivity Statistics* (database) in *OECD Economic Surveys,* http://dx.doi.org/10.1787/16097513.

OECD (2017i), "Latvia", in *Economic Policy Reforms 2017: Going for Growth*, OECD Publishing, Paris, http://dx.doi.org/10.1787/growth-2017-34-en.

OECD (2016a), "Latvia", in *OECD Economic Outlook, Volume 2016 Issue 2*, OECD Publishing, Paris, http://dx.doi.org/10.1787/eco_outlook-v2016-2-31-en.

OECD (2016b), *OECD Reviews of Labour Market and Social Policies: Latvia 2016*, OECD Publishing, Paris, http://dx.doi.org/10.1787/9789264250505-en.

OECD (2016c), "Labour force participation rate, by sex and age group", *OECD.Stat* (database), http://stats.oecd.org/index.aspx?queryid=54753.

OECD (2016d), "Female share of seats on boards of the largest publicly listed companies", *OECD.Stat* (database), http://stats.oecd.org/index.aspx?queryid=54753.

OECD (2016e), *Economic Policy Reforms 2016: Going for Growth Interim Report*, OECD Publishing, Paris, http://dx.doi.org/10.1787/growth-2016-en.

OECD (2015a), *Government at a Glance 2015, Country Fact Sheet, Latvia,* www.oecd.org/gov/Latvia.pdf.

OECD (2015b), *OECD Economic Surveys: Latvia 2015*, OECD Publishing, Paris, http://dx.doi.org/10.1787/9789264228467-en.

OECD (2015c), *Policy Framework for Investment, 2015 Edition*, OECD Publishing, Paris, http://dx.doi.org/10.1787/9789264208667-en.

OECD (2015d), *Equal Access to Justice, OECD Expert Roundtable, Background notes*, 7 October 2015, www.oecd.org/gov/Equal-Access-Justice-Roundtable-background-note.pdf.

OECD (2015e), *All on Board: Making Inclusive Growth Happen*, OECD Publishing, Paris, http://dx.doi.org/10.1787/9789264218512-en.

OECD (2015f), *Towards Inclusive Growth – Access to Justice: Supporting people-focused justice services* (flyer), www.oecd.org/gov/access-to-justice-supporting-people-focused-justice-services.pdf.

OECD (2014a), *Annual Report on the OECD* Guidelines *for Multinational Enterprises 2014: Responsible Business Conduct by Sector*, OECD Publishing, Paris, http://dx.doi.org/10.1787/mne-2014-en.

OECD (2014b), *Kazakhstan: Review of the Central Administration*, OECD Publishing, Paris, http://dx.doi.org/10.1787/9789264224605-en.

OECD (2013), "What makes civil justice effective?", *OECD Economics Department Policy Notes*, No. 18, June 2013, www.oecd.org/eco/growth/Civil%20Justice%20Policy%20Note.pdf.

OECD (2010a), *Competitiveness and Private Sector Development: Egypt 2010: Business Climate Development Strategy*, OECD Publishing, Paris, http://dx.doi.org/10.1787/9789264087408-en.

OECD/IMCO (2013), *Strengthening Evidence-based Policy Making on Security and Justice in Mexico*, OECD Publishing, Paris, http://dx.doi.org/10.1787/9789264190450-en.

US Department of State (2017), *Investment Climate Statements for 2017, Latvia,* www.state.gov/e/eb/rls/othr/ics/investmentclimatestatements/index.htm?year=2017&dlid=269918#wrapper (accessed 30 January 2018).

World Bank (2018), "Ease of doing business in Latvia", *Doing Business Indicators*, www.doingbusiness.org/data/exploreeconomies/latvia.

World Economic Forum (2016), *The Global Competitiveness Report 2016–2017,* www3.weforum.org/docs/GCR2016-2017/05FullReport/TheGlobalCompetitivenessReport2016-2017_FINAL.pdf (accessed 30 January 2018).

Chapter 2. Responding to business needs: Fostering a doing-business enabling framework in Latvia

This chapter presents and discusses the current organisational and procedural arrangements deployed by the government to pursue administrative simplification and promote an increasingly business-friendly environment in Latvia. By placing specific focus on procedures regulated by the Latvian Commercial Law, the chapter seeks to identify actions that could further facilitate doing business based on evidential validation drawn from the Chapter 3 related to costs associated with administrative procedures.

The legal and regulatory framework for conducting business in Latvia

The general legal and policy framework

The Latvian Commercial Law is at the centre of founding, operating and closing businesses in Latvia. It applies to sole traders, partnerships (in particular, general and limited partnerships) and companies (in particular, private and public companies). The Commercial Law establishes the rules for starting a business, registration requirements, organisational and financial management, the relationship between members, adaptions and restructurings, and the liquidation of a commercial entity. In its application to commercial reality the Commercial Law works in conjunction with, and refers to, other laws such as the Law on the Enterprise Registry,[1] the Law on Annual Financial Statements and Consolidated Financial Statements[2] and the Law on Electronic Documents.[3]

The Commercial Law was adopted on 13 April 2000 and has since been amended several times. The number of amendments is particularly high since 2011 and it is not unusual to see up to four amendments per year as, for example, in 2013. Historically, the Commercial Law was built on the experience of its German counterpart, the *Handelsgesetzbuch* of 1897.[4] This is still visible in both the structure and specific provisions of the law. The Latvian Commercial Law deviates insofar as it integrates the rules concerning private and public companies into one formal law. As a result, the Commercial Law contains a section on general rules applying to all company forms and more specific rules applying to private and public companies only.

The country's accession to the European Union (EU) in 2004 proved to have a high impact on the regulation of businesses in Latvia. The Commercial Law reflects the European Union's *acquis* to commercial and company law. A certain degree of harmonisation and cross-border compatibility strengthened the international dimension of Latvian commercial and company law. The standardisation effect of the EU directives is particularly felt with regard to public companies, while the Latvian legislation is little constrained by EU law with regard to private companies.

The Law on Judicial Power regulates the judicial system in Latvia.[5] It introduced a three-tier courts system and laid down basic principles maintaining judicial independence. The procedures for hearing cases are outlined in the Civil Procedure Law,[6] the Criminal Procedural Law[7] and the Administrative Procedure Law.[8] In Latvia the Constitutional Court operates as an independent institution examining laws' conformity with the Constitution. Latvia is reforming the judicial map and consolidating small district city court areas within the jurisdiction of regional courts (OECD, 2017). The reform aims to improve the efficiency of the court system through the equalisation of the length of the proceedings, ensuring equal practices before the court and redistribution of judges' posts.

In parallel, the government adopted a range of regulatory policies and frameworks to encourage a sound business environment and economic development. The National Development Plan 2014-2020 is the highest level strategic mid-term document currently in force, approved by the *Saeima* in December 2012 (Government of Latvia, 2012). It includes, among other things, a list of regulatory policy-related priorities focusing mostly on impact assessment, administrative burden reduction and regulatory simplification as well as the better engagement of stakeholders.

The National Development Plan complements the National Reform Programme of Latvia in the implementation of the "EU 2020" Strategy,[9] of which one of the key policy action lines of Latvia's national economy is the improvement of its business environment, envisaging the simplification of administrative procedures, the elimination of administrative costs and burden, and the implementation of e-services for the performers of economic activities.

In 2016, the government set the overall goal of placing Latvia among the top 20 economies in the World Bank's "Doing Business" rating and among the top 40 economies in the Global Competitiveness Index in 2018.[10]

While the regulatory policy of the Latvian government is not consolidated in a single, overarching document, several individual elements of the better regulation agenda are spelt out in strategies and programmatic documents at both governmental and ministerial level – a number of which are presented in the various sections of this chapter. The institutional stakeholders responsible for the implementation of the different aspects of the commercial and regulatory policy framework are highlighted in Box 2.1.

Box 2.1. Institutional responsibility for commercial and regulatory policy in Latvia

Responsibility for commercial and regulatory policy in the Latvian government is allocated among several institutional stakeholders, as follows.

The State Chancellery

At the centre of government, the State Chancellery is in charge of several elements of the better regulation agenda. The Chancellery's main tasks include activities to mainstream and upgrade regulatory impact analysis (RIA), such as extending the scope of impacts to be assessed and revising the RIA Handbook. The Chancellery is also actively promoting capacity building on RIA, with the implementation, moreover, of two pilot exercises to test possible methodologies and procedures.

The Chancellery is also responsible for the development of a new Public Administration Reform Plan, which will cover initiatives related to both reducing administrative burdens and the Open Government Partnership. With regard to cutting red tape, the Chancellery launched a website via which stakeholders and citizens can report cases for potential simplification and internal surveys on regulation-inside-government bottlenecks (notably in relation to data sharing).

The Ministry of Justice

In Latvia, the Ministry of Justice plays a critical role in setting a commercial framework and providing a range of services to business. It provides the other public administration institutions with methodological assistance in the development of draft regulations. It is the body co-ordinating and overseeing the transposition of EU legislation into national legislation. It is, moreover, directly responsible for the elaboration and implementation of policies related to, among other things, state law, administrative law, civil law, commercial law, thereby having a direct impact on economic activities.

The Ministry of Economy

The Ministry of Economy's main involvement in the Latvian better regulation agenda concerns the simplification of the regulatory framework for business. On the basis of sustained and close dialogue with businesses and entrepreneurs, since 1999 the ministry has managed the related "Action Plan for the Improvement of the Business Environment", which over the years listed several hundreds of measures to relieve business from disproportionate administrative barriers. The ministry is also responsible for reducing the number of licenses and permits and for progressively shifting from an *ex ante* authorisation regime to an *ex post*, risk-based inspection system.

The Ministry of Environmental Protection and Regional Development

The Ministry of Environmental Protection and Regional Development is the leading state authority for e-government and the information society, working also at the regional and local levels. Within the ministry, the Public Services Department deals with the planning of electronic services (such as e-identity, e-documents and e-signature) as well as with the related infrastructure. The same department is also in charge of the implementation of the one-stop-shop principle. The technical aspects of information and communication technology (ICT) development and management are managed by the Electronic Government Department.

The State Regional Development Agency (SRDA) operates under the supervision of the ministry. Originally tasked with administrating programmes for entrepreneurs in specially supported territories and implementing various state and EU Structural Fund-financed local municipality support programmes, SRDA's current main task is to provide e-services for governmental and municipal institutions.[11]

Cross-Sectoral Coordination Centre

Under the umbrella of the Prime Minister of Latvia, the Cross-Sectoral Coordination Centre (CSCC)'s main role is to supervise and co-ordinate development planning by allowing for cross-level co-operation in the decision-making process. In this respect, the CSCC is entrusted with developing and monitoring the implementation of the National Development Plan of Latvia for 2014-2020, the Sustainable Development Strategy of Latvia until 2030 and the national development programmes pertaining to the country's involvement in the European Union. Moreover, the CSCC is in charge of co-ordinating the corporate governance of state-owned enterprises (SOEs) operating in a partially centralised SOE governance co-ordination model.

Source: Information gathered by the OECD from government sources during the OECD fact-finding mission, October 2017; Latvia - Cross-Sectoral Coordination Centre, website.

The Commercial Law: A facilitative commercial framework for all

Businesses consulted for this report expressed their general satisfaction with the Latvian Commercial Law. The legal forms of businesses offered and their general design provides a reliable framework as the basis for their commercial activity. The stakeholders also expressed their general satisfaction with the public services involved in operationalising the Commercial Law and its associated substantive and procedural laws and institutions, such as the Enterprise Registry, the State Land Service and Land Registry offices and Patent Office (see below).

One of the issues mentioned by stakeholders concerns the spirit of application of the Commercial Law and its related laws. It is felt that state institutions such as courts and public services take a rather restrictive approach in commercial reality. Where, for example, the Commercial Law does not provide a rule for a specific issue, the state institutions' starting point may not always be the stakeholders' freedom to privately create rights and obligations as they see fit. Instead courts and public services conclude, at times, that when a matter is not regulated, it is not allowed. This is thought to contradict the history of the Commercial Law, which was enacted to facilitate business and which should view prohibition as the exception and not as the starting point. At least two solutions were proposed by stakeholders:

First, by establishing an enabling culture by principles of interpretation, where for instance the higher courts, in particular the Supreme Court, could contribute to a more facilitative interpretation of the law in their judgement. Second, the legislature could support this cultural change by selected intervention where practice and courts do not achieve facilitative solutions.

An issue for further discussion might be bringing state enterprises and institutions with a commercial function, such as certain ports by way of example, within the general framework of Commercial Law if not already the case. This might unleash the beneficial effects of a facilitative Commercial Law in two ways. The established structures of the Commercial Law – for example the organisational rules of private and public companies – could be an efficient backbone to organise such enterprises and institutions.[12] Further, private enterprises might find a levelled playing field with state-owned enterprises, contributing to a higher efficiency of the Latvian economy. To give an example, the Port of Hamburg is legally organised as a public company (*Hamburger Hafen und Logistik Aktiengesellschaft*). This contributes to a successful governance structure and allowed for a part-privatisation by way of publicly offering the shares on the Frankfurt Stock Exchange in 2007 (with the state keeping a majority share).[13]

Adapting to modern forms of business

Stakeholders strongly highlighted the need to adapt the Commercial Law to modern forms of business. According to them, the law did not follow all modern developments, resulting in gaps in the law. One example is the provision of a reliable framework for modern forms of business finance, including but not limited to start-up funding and crowdfunding. At times, however, very specific new rules were added to the Commercial Law such as those on leasing and franchising in 2008. Consequently, the Commercial Law today presents itself as a mix of general rules, more specific rules and a number of gaps compared to modern business reality. Stakeholders emphasised that this should not necessarily be understood as a general call for hard law regulation. Instead, soft law and self-regulation could be considered as alternatives (Box 2.2). An approach to law reform that is more based on thorough research and economic impact assessments was called for. This was seen to be more beneficial in the end than regulation based on anecdotal calls from stakeholders.

Box 2.2. Getting the regulatory mix right

A general policy for selecting the types of rules for a modern commercial law framework ensures the right regulatory mix, whereby the regulatory instruments used are compatible and enhance each other if combined. According to the OECD *Guiding Principles for Regulatory Quality and Performance* adopted by the OECD Council in 2005, regulatory mix fosters "innovation though market incentives and goal-based approaches" and is in line with "competition, trade investment-facilitating principles at domestic and international levels." Such a general policy therefore prevents combinations of methods that are incompatible and allows for an informed and improved policy outcome involving a mix of the following regulatory instruments :

- mandatory statutory law
- non-mandatory statutory law
- ministerial orders
- soft law (such as a corporate governance code)
- self-regulation by commercial actors
- freedom of contract.

Note: For more information on the regulatory mix (with examples from mediation), see International Finance Corporation (2016).
Source: International Finance Corporation (2016); Cunningham, N. and Sinclair, D. (1999); OECD Guiding Principles for Regulatory Quality and Performance.

Toward legal certainty and the predictability of the Commercial Law

Consultation

This report is a testament to the Ministry of Justice's articulate consultation culture, similar to that found in many other OECD countries (Box 2.3). Involving stakeholders systematically and inclusively brings a number of advantages. It provides legislative bodies with a full picture of the regulatory challenge and, in particular, exposes conflicts of interest between groups of stakeholders that need consideration. It also improves acceptance and compliance with reform projects. If all stakeholders are involved at an early stage, their acceptance of the resulting laws is higher even if their wishes are not met as they may deem the process fair. Early involvement also raises awareness within the relevant groups. This has the positive effect of a quicker adoption of the mandated changes by both public and private actors.

Box 2.3. Consultation mechanisms in some OECD countries

The Australian government established the Business Consultation website to improve dialogue between business and government. The website provides state departments and agencies with an opportunity to consult business-related policy or regulation with various stakeholders. Businesses, individuals, industry associations and non-profit organisations can register and participate in the consultation processes. The government conducts public or direct consultations. A public consultation is available to all parties interested while a direct one is private and sent to selected stakeholders. The website aims to reduce the regulatory burden on Australian business and deliver better outcomes by consulting early in the policy development process.

Many other OECD member countries (e.g. France, Greece, Luxembourg, Portugal, and Spain) consult social partners and civil society including business groups through the Economic and Social Councils. For instance, in Portugal the Conselho Económico e Social (CSE) was created in 1991 based on provisions of the Constitution. Its mission is to advise the government, promote the involvement of economic and social players in the government's decision-making process, and provide a forum for dialogue between social partners and other civil society organisations. In the course of this work the CSE draws up opinions on draft legislation and economic policy programmes submitted to it by the government or on its own initiative. Members include representatives of the government, workers' and employers' organisations, the autonomous regions and municipalities, as well as representatives of civil society (such as professionals, researchers and universities, consumer and environment associations, universities).

Source: Australia - Government Initiative Business Consultation (n.d.); OECD (2010).

Stakeholders expressed their content with the sincere openness of the Latvian state institutions in considering their regulatory concerns and including them in drafting commercial reform laws. Some stakeholders, however, felt that the inclusion of stakeholders' views could be more systematic and organised. In addition, some stakeholders expressed that there might be an overemphasis on listening to the voices of entrepreneurs while other stakeholders such as judges and academics might receive less consideration.

Pace of reform and uncertainty

Modern governments, in particular in the European Union, face the challenge of finding the right balance between speedy reactions to reform needs and avoiding overburdening institutions and actors with a hectic rhythm of reform. This challenge finds its roots in multiple causes. To name a few: the European Union adds a second source of reform needs in addition to national reform initiatives; moreover, information technology (IT) and globalisation have accelerated change in the business world, which needs to be reflected in the underlying law.

As described above, the Commercial Law is at the centre of founding, operating and closing businesses in Latvia as well as addressing any related disputes. While going in the right direction, there is a widespread feeling from state institutions such as courts and services as well as from entrepreneurs that the hectic rhythm of law or regulation reforms is difficult to follow. In 2016, the most commonly mentioned obstacle impeding business growth was "frequent changes in laws and regulations" (mentioned by 66% of respondents) (Figure 2.1). This can have an impact on legal stability and predictability, hindering business development. Some small and medium-sized enterprises (SMEs) that do not have legal resources may also feel overwhelmed and have trouble keeping up to date.

Figure 2.1. Obstacles hindering business activities in Latvia, 2001-16

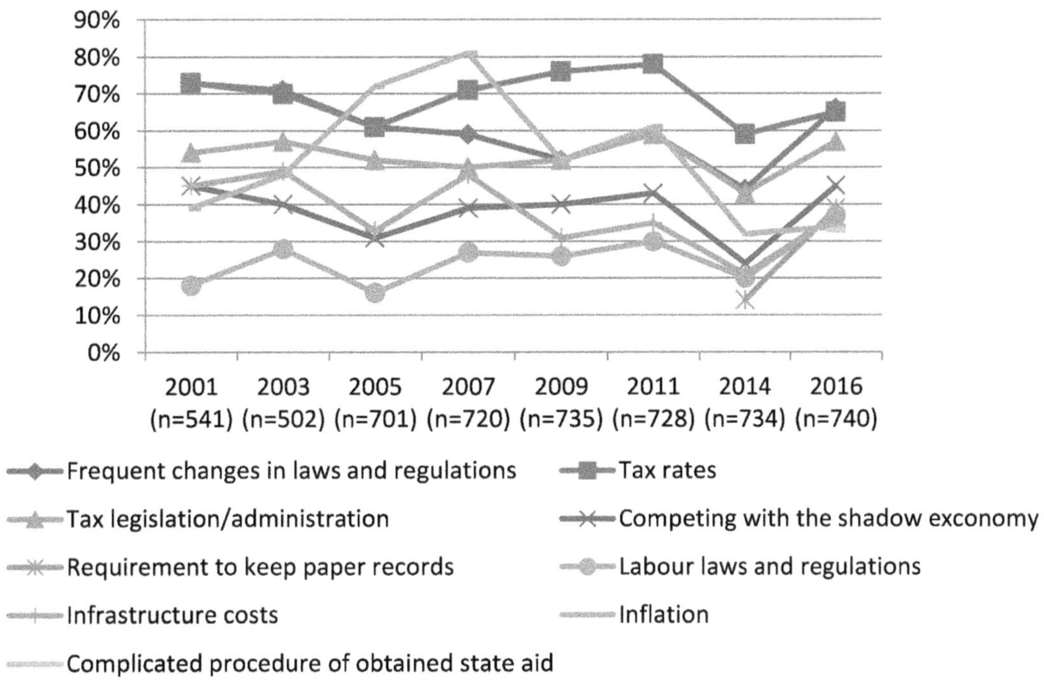

Source: Adapted from Latvia - Ministry of Economy (2016).

A possible solution might be to collect reform amendments and enact reform packages in less hasty waves. In addition, while there are initiatives to communicate laws and regulations in understandable language to businesses, there seems to be room for improvement. Improving further the communication of reform packages, in particular explaining their key measures and principles, might make it easier for those concerned to digest the new information. Currently, Latvian law and essential websites are not consistently available for foreign investors in an up-to-date and English version. Some stakeholders suggested that allowing accounting and employment documents to be provided in English, which currently seems prohibited, would increase the attractiveness of Latvia as a place for foreign investment.

Access to law and legal information in a globalised world

Entrepreneurs and managers praised recent initiatives to communicate laws and regulations in accessible language. As mentioned above, widening the horizon in order to attract more international investment might be a strong reason to extend these measures further and consider the needs of investors from outside of Latvia. A core initiative could be to make Latvian law and essential websites consistently available for foreign investors in an up-to-date English version. In some countries, e.g. Estonia, all current Estonian laws are available in a consolidated English version, the English version being informative only. In the United Kingdom, information is provided based on business lifecycle events (Box 2.4). A point for discussion would be whether stakeholders should have the option to choose another language such as English to be the legally relevant language for company, accounting and employment documents. The guiding question would be whether the expected advantages of more international investment and improved cross-border co-operation would outweigh the public cost of providing this option.

Box 2.4. Providing information for business by lifecycle events

Many countries design and organise information systems and explain business law by way of practical topics. For instance, the UK web portal, gov.uk, provides information on government services, including a bookmark for business and the self-employed (see below). The Irish portal helps to identify the main regulations which affect businesses and provides links to the relevant agencies and their guidance, tools and contact points.

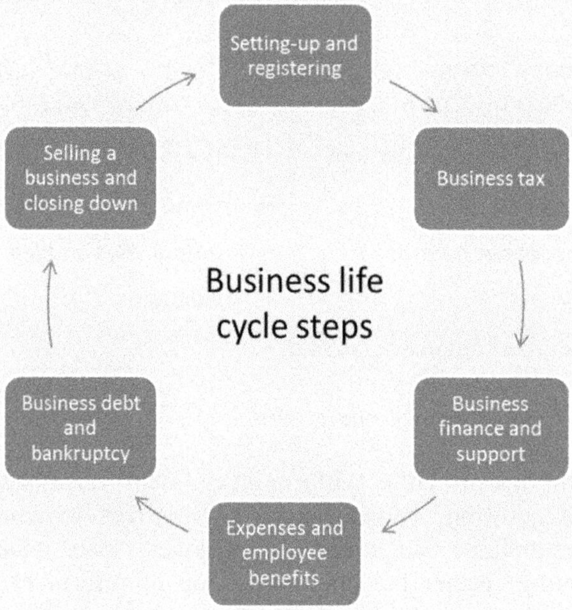

Source: UK - gov.uk, "Business and self-employed", website; Ireland – Department of Business, Enterprise and Innovation, website.

The formal requirements for businesses: Reduction and coherence

Notaries and electronic means of identification

Many stakeholders raised the issue of reducing the formal requirements regarding documents to be submitted to the Enterprise Registry. This concerns namely Sections 9, 10, 25, 187 and 327 of the Commercial Law. In particular, a larger number of stakeholders called for a reduction or even abolition of the need to provide documents in notarised form. Other stakeholders, in particular sworn notaries,[14] raised reasons to keep such requirements or to reshape them and make them fit for the future. Reducing formal requirements should not be seen in isolation: attempts to reduce costs for businesses need to be considered against the background of introducing electronic forms of documents and identification as well as against the background of the practical readiness of such electronic solutions (see Chapter 2). Further, reform of the formal requirements should happen with a clear vision of the purpose such rules will serve and under consideration of the institutions that will administer the requirements. It is suggested that the reduction of formal requirements and the introduction of electronic solutions provide immense potential to reduce costs and create benefits for businesses. However, relevant reform calls for a measured and integrated manner. Care needs to be taken to include all stakeholders. Against this background, the following text concentrates on principles and core issues.

For historical reasons, Latvia involves notaries in the formal procedure of submitting documents to the Enterprise Registry. Latvian law, however, developed quite a specific way in which notaries are involved by the Commercial Law. According to Section 9(1) Sentence 4 of the Commercial Law, if the signature of a person must be notarised, there are three alternative options to comply with this requirement: 1) certification by a sworn notary; 2) certification by an official of the Enterprise Registry; or 3) a secure electronic signature if it is a document in electronic form. This rule gives businesses a choice, in particular between certification by a sworn notary or by an official of the register. Compared to the officials of the Enterprise Registry (state notaries), sworn notaries apply stricter rules.[15] This leads to more substantive checks by sworn notaries, but it also makes the procedure more cumbersome for users. As a result, it is more attractive for applicants to go to the state notaries/officials in the Enterprise Registry rather than the sworn notaries, since the requirements before the state notaries/officials in the Enterprise Registry are lower.

Compared to other jurisdictions that involve notaries in commercial law matters (e.g. Germany), the function of notaries in Latvian commercial matters is quite limited. Latvian commercial law does not require notaries to check the legal substance of events or documents to be registered. Rather the function of notaries is generally limited to certifying the identity of persons acting in the relevant matter. Consequently, essential acts of notaries are: 1) determining the person's identity (comparing the person, the ID card and the register of people);[16] 2) checking the validity of documents;[17] 3) verifying the capacity of persons to act; 4) in cases of representation checking the authorisation (based on the power of attorney and register entries, e.g. Registry of revoked power of attorneys). For example, a notary can be involved in checking a person's identity when registering a business or in certifying the identity of persons party to a share transfer. The sworn notaries representatives involved in the stakeholder interviews estimated that 85% to 90% of their work relates to certifying identities, while the remaining time covers work dealing with the substance of legal acts.

By contrast, in Germany, another country with a history of notarial involvement in commercial law matters, notaries are more involved in checking the substance matter of documents to be registered. They are, for example, more substantively involved in verifying the articles of association and share transfer contracts. It is noted, though, that German law does not provide for alternatives to notarial certification as does Latvian law. Rather, where notaries are to be involved, there is no other optional form.

English law, on the other hand, does not rely on notaries to certify commercial documents to be registered. Instead, the relevant functions are achieved by a combination of prescribed forms, the involvement of the companies and the relevant register (Companies House). The fact that jurisdictions such as the English administer the same functions without notarial certification can raise the question that unnecessary costs are borne by Latvian businesses without achieving a corresponding advantage.

In recent times, notarial involvement in commercial matters came under additional pressure by electronic means of identification in procedural matters. E-signatures, e-identities and other electronic forms offer a cost-efficient way to identify actors. In addition, these forms of identification correspond with the transfer of registers from paper-based to IT-based organisation (see below).

Against this background, two different opinions emerged in the stakeholder interviews. On the one hand, various stakeholders believed that some or all of the provisions requiring notarised certification in the Commercial Law could be abolished. This was often tied with the suggestion to improve and widen the use of electronic means for identification under the Commercial Law. In particular, it was thought that if e-signatures or e-identities ensured identification, notarial identification was not necessary any longer. This was connected with the suggestion to use e-identification not only for communication with public services such as the Enterprise Registry, but also for other types of communication such as business-to-business (B2B) communication. The idea of having a proper company e-address was supported in this context. It was added that fraud prevention by way of analysing electronic data delivers stronger results than the visual checks carried out by notaries. Overall, simplifying the registration process for one-person companies was also seen as necessary.

On the other hand, sworn notaries maintained that their involvement is still required in the interest of fraud prevention. They argued that electronic means of identification are vulnerable to abuse because no one checks whether the relevant electronic device is operated by the person who pretends to operate it. In addition, sworn notaries argued that one of the reasons why businesses register in Estonia rather than in Latvia is the fact that Estonian notaries are more substantially involved in checking documents, thus lending more credibility to the Estonian registration system. Since no formal risk management system is currently in place in the Latvian state administration to carry out *ex post* controls on the submitted documentation, the notarisation requirement serves as an *ex ante* filter. At the same time, given that notaries verify and certify the validity of the signature and identity without performing a substantive check of documents signed casts doubts on the effectiveness of the measure to prevent crime.

Latvian sworn notaries are preparing themselves for the future: they are currently investing in IT systems such that certification can be done at a distance (e.g. facial recognition using video conferencing), supported by recent law reform aimed at facilitating notarial services. Foreign investors in particular might benefit from these changes. In the opinion of the sworn notaries, the legislature should focus on what and why notaries should be involved in, and limit the powers of institutions involved in the same process, i.e. sworn and state notaries.[18] As part of the next steps it will be important to consider the associated costs (or, conversely, the associated potential benefits) associated with notarisation (also based on the burden analysis developed further below; Chapter 3 addresses the possible simplification of the registration procedure by streamlining notarisation).

Administrative simplification for business development

In Latvia, initiatives aimed at simplifying the regulatory and administrative framework have traditionally been driven by a business-oriented rationale. Improving the business environment is an ongoing reform endeavour by the Latvian government.

Contrary to most OECD countries, Latvia has not carried out a larger programme on *ex post* measurement of administrative burdens. The Latvian government has rather opted for a more qualitative approach based on a sustained and systematic dialogue with stakeholders. The approach seems to be delivering tangible results, contributing to steadily improving the country's performance over the past few years. The approach is also generally viewed positively by the representatives of the private sector and the public administration bodies.

Besides the direct inputs from the affected stakeholders, priority simplification measures are identified on the basis of Latvia's ranking in the World Bank's Doing Business Indicators and the World Economic Forum's Global Competitiveness Index, which are permanent target benchmarks of the Government Declaration and the National Development Plan for 2014-2020 for the achievement of an excellent business environment. The government also intends to benchmark its progress through the European Innovation Scoreboard as of 2018.

The Action Plan for Improvement of the Business Environment

The longest standing and arguably most significant initiative undertaken by the government to ease doing business in Latvia is the Action Plan for Improvement of the Business Environment (the "Action Plan"), elaborated yearly since 1999 by the Ministry of Economy in co-operation with stakeholders: the National Economic Council, the Foreign Investors Council in Latvia, the Latvian Chamber of Commerce and Industry, and the Employers' Confederation of Latvia.

The Action Plan lists concrete measures aimed at eliminating excessive regulatory burdens in all areas related to running a business. Over the years, several hundreds of such measures were identified and introduced as a part of the plan.

The Action Plan currently being implemented, issued in February 2017, seeks to achieve "simple and high-quality services in business: more e-services". In particular, Action Lines 2.1. and 3.11. explicitly cover *Starting a business* and *Smart public administration and its e-services*, respectively – two set of reforms directly addressed in this chapter. Overall, the Action Plan includes 46 measures, reflecting the following paradigms:

- observing the one-stop-shop principle
- implementing the "Consult First" principle, especially at the stage of starting a business
- simple and qualitative state public e-services – even more active integration of e-solutions (digitalisation)
- introducing business-environment-friendly infrastructure development services, including introducing and observing reasonable deadlines ensuring the importance of safety and quality requirements
- simplifying administrative requirements, especially in the field of taxes and accounting, and reducing the bureaucratic burden
- strengthening the legitimate expectations in the regulatory framework, especially in matters of protection of rights of investors and insolvency.[19]

Box 2.5. Latvia's Action Plan for Improvement of Business Environment 2017: Main objectives

The Action Plan issued in February 2017 includes the following main objectives:

Starting a business

- Transition to the company's registration online only starting from 2018
- Reducing the standard costs for company's e-registration to EUR 100
- Dealing with construction permits
- Providing all construction co-ordination processes digitally only not later than in 2020
- Implementing the silent consent principle in the process of co-ordination of construction intention
- Improving the insurance system in the construction field.

Protecting investors

- Reviewing the stock option framework, granting shareholders the right to waive the pre-emptive right if new shares are issued, simplified reorganisation process, etc.

Resolving insolvency

- Creation of a monitoring system of insolvency proceedings that could indicate main problem areas.

Efficient public administration and e-services

- Integration of the "Consult First" principle in the government's work
- Improving the business section of the Public Administration Service Portal (www.latvija.lv)
- Providing at least 20 new e-services on the Public Administration Service Portal over three years
- Providing roadmaps for new entrepreneurs
- Implementing the silent consent principle in several certification proceedings, as well as in other procedures.

Paying taxes

- Ensuring the use of a single account for all tax payments.

Source: Latvia - Ministry of Economy.

The measures fall under the portfolio and responsibilities of several ministries. The implementation of the Action Plan and the respect of the targets and deadlines defined therein is hence decentralised, with rather soft co-ordination and oversight powers entrusted to the Ministry of Economy. In case of significant delays and lack of progress, political discussions take place at the ministerial level.

To date, ministries have not yet fully deployed quantification methodologies such as the Standard Cost Model (or equivalent), grounding their simplification programmes on qualitative assessments and perception surveys. One established source of information in this respect is the portal *Let's Share Burden Together!*, which offers citizens and businesses the opportunity to report excessive administrative burdens and submit proposals for simplification (OECD, 2016).[20] The reports submitted through the website are considered by the State Chancellery, which decides whether or not to organise a follow-up or not, in co-ordination with the responsible state body. In the future, the portal will be also used as a platform to conduct more targeted sector- and policy-specific opinion surveys on administrative burden and bureaucracy.[21]

In addition, every other year a business survey, "The Impact of Administrative Procedures on Business Environment" is conducted to collect inputs from the stakeholders on perceived barriers to doing business and on trends further to the simplification agenda.

The Draft Public Administration Reform Plan 2020

Most recently, and in the wake of implementing the National Development Plan 2014-2020, a Draft Public Administration Reform Plan 2020 ("PA Reform Plan") was announced at the State Secretaries Meeting of 27 July 2017, and is currently being finalised.[22] The Public Administration Reform Plan will complement the Ministry of Economy Action Plan for Improvement of the Business Environment. It was drawn up in light of the ever-increasing public demand for the efficiency and competitiveness of public administration, the simplification of processes and the reduction of administrative burdens.

The programme for reforms outlined in the PA Reform Plan takes account of the processes, functions and human resources available in the Latvian public administration. It grounds future actions on the three dimensions of "economy" (investing less), "utility" (investing proportionally, taking account of the benefits) and "efficiency" (investing smartly). The resulting initiatives are not supposed to increase state budget expenditures. Rather, reforms should be carried forward thanks to innovative solutions that rationalise Latvia's administrative regime.

In the PA Reform Plan, the Latvian government identifies a number of recurring structural challenges, including:[23]

- The public administration and human resource development policy is currently not sufficiently flexible and is incapable of adapting to the rapidly changing environment and public interest.
- The allocation of responsibilities and tasks to discharge administrative functions is not efficient and does not sufficiently leverage synergies and economies of scale, causing significant internal administrative burden and consumption of human resources.
- The system does not stimulate individual responsibility. Performance appraisals could be further grounded on a clearly defined reporting system with established criteria. Remunerations in the public administration, moreover, are not competitive and contribute to a negative public image of the public administration and a continuous flow of senior management into the private sector.

To tackle these challenges, the PA Reform Plan sets up ten reform directions, which should be implemented over a period of three years and are intended to be the basis for changing the culture of the state administration. Among the reform priorities, the government seeks to introduce a "zero bureaucracy" approach, facilitating the transition to a small and analytical public administration with streamlined supervisory and control functions (Box 2.6).

Box 2.6. The "zero bureaucracy" target in the Draft Public Administration Reform Plan 2020

Priority Action 8 of the Draft Public Administration Reform Plan 2020 seeks to leverage better regulation policy and strengthen efficiency and effectiveness audits to minimise administrative burdens. Abiding by the principles of "regulating as little as possible" and "intervening only where necessary", the government seeks to promote a transparent, evidence-based decision-making process by engaging more with the public and being more responsive.

Regular online public surveys on "Reducing burden together" are expected to identify areas of disproportionate bureaucracy affecting businesses and citizens. The proposed creation of a "Zero Bureaucracy" project team should contribute to developing effective simplification solutions. Initiatives already launched on inter-institutional administrative bottlenecks will continue operating, with a view to reducing the frequency of different administrative procedures and reporting.

State administration managers also play an important role in reducing administrative burdens and supporting internal audit function. Implementing horizontal audits and switching from compliance to performance reviews should help improve efficiency and economy.

Source: Latvia - Draft Public Administration Plan 2020, p. 28.

"Consult First"

One of the most visible, innovative and successful measures implemented in the framework story of the government's administrative simplification programme is the so-called "Consult First" project signed in June 2017. Explicitly drawing from OECD guidance,[24] this initiative led by the Minister of Economy is a co-operation between 22 state market surveillance and enforcement bodies[25] as well as business associations including representatives of the Latvian Employers' Confederation, the Latvian Chamber of Commerce and Industry, the Latvian Traders Association and the Association of Latvian Food Traders.

It aims to encourage a "client-oriented" approach to promote self-assessment and advice on compliance and conformity correction, prior to proceeding to established sanctions. The "Consult First" principle aims to provide advice first, before sanctioning businesses, to some extent. Legal rules that are considered essential will still be enforced without prior advice. In order to ensure uniform application of the "Consult First" principle, the Ministry of Economy introduced specific guidelines to the enforcement authorities, and linkages are envisaged with revised performance appraisals and capacity-building programmes. Consultations and communication are thereby put at the forefront of the dialogue with businesses, limiting recourse to fines to severe and recidivist cases.

Box 2.7. "Consult First" in Latvia: A good practice for doing business simplification

The Latvian "Consult First" project did not require amendments to the existing legal base. It will be implemented following two main pillars, outlined in the Ministry of Economy's guidelines:

- The first refers to the "efficiency of the surveillance activities", and includes drawing up the authority strategy for effective surveillance; establishing key performance indicators (KPI); following a risk-based approach in surveillance activities; and gearing the activities towards the new overarching objective, namely to achieve compliance.
- The second set of measures is about instilling a "client-based approach in regulatory practice". This includes organising the provision of information and advice; the deployment of appropriate methods to explain the applicable requirements (including IT solutions); considering specifically the needs of new businesses; developing a service-oriented culture within the authority; and running client satisfaction evaluations of the work and achievements.

Criteria will be drawn up to evaluate progress among the authorities with regard to introducing the principle in their daily work. The first results of the evaluation are expected in 2018. The authorities will be ranked according to their compliance with the guidelines, and recommendations for improvement will be made for the following year.

The "Consult First" project is expected to run until 2020, when a comprehensive evaluation will be carried out. Albeit at its early stage, a number of success factors can already be identified, which make the Latvian experience with this innovative approach an international good practice. They include:

- the strong political backing given to the project by the Prime Minister, making it a government flagship initiative
- the shared ownership of the project, triggered not least by the fact that good practices already developed in some inspectorates were leveraged and consolidated in the elaboration of the general approach (bottom-up and horizontal approach to reform design) as well as thanks to the intense consultation with business representatives (participatory approach)
- the comprehensive (whole-of-government) nature of the project, which touches upon various dimensions: from incentives included in the civil service reform (amendments of relevant KPIs to evaluation inspectors) to partnerships with the Public Administration School to launch new, dedicated capacity programmes), as well as – as it is envisaged – other levels of government with the future involvement of the Latvian municipalities
- the very constructive and responsible attitude taken by the private sector, which did not limit itself to sheer complaining but contributed to ideas and improvements on their end
- drawing lessons from international experiences with reforming enforcement governance and deploying mechanisms to stimulate compliance, thanks also to the good practices shared by the OECD.

Source: See https://em.gov.lv/files/ministrija/konsultevispirms/2017-06-15_10_05_37_KV_Vadlinijas_FINAL_MAKETS_14.06.2017.pdf.

This approach is highly welcomed by businesses and serves as a useful addition to the repertoire of state agencies dealing with businesses. Stakeholders proposed two points to further improve the "Consult First" principle. First, stakeholders asked whether further clarity in terms of what is key (immediate enforcement) and what is non-key (consult first) can be achieved. Second, stakeholders suggested establishing the "Consult First" initiative as a right for businesses as opposed to a discretionary remedy of the state agency. Further analysis is needed to assess the impact of such requests.

Further reform initiatives

The government also envisages launching additional initiatives that may be conducive to making further progress on administrative simplification for improving the business environment, primarily under the leadership and co-ordination of the State Chancellery. Among such initiatives are:

- Newly established, dedicated *Labs*, which should help investigate ways to enhance ethics in the public administration, and embed results-oriented and performance management practices.
- An *Entrepreneurship Project*, to be carried out as of 2018 in conjunction with the Latvian Public Administration School, which aims to diffuse end user and entrepreneur-centred approaches to decision making among Latvian regulators.[26]
- In the framework of the European Structural and Investment Funds (ESIF) project, a *single portal*[27] as of 2020 to elaborate and co-ordinate legal acts within the executive branch. The portal will also include the "Public Participation" e-service, which will publish white and green papers to gather opinions from civil society and the public sector; announce stakeholder engagement activities, and consolidate inputs and feedback received in various consultation rounds.

An evidence-based regulatory process

As mentioned in the previous section, Latvia put less emphasis on quantifying administrative burdens during stock-taking simplification reviews than in the process of elaborating new regulatory interventions. Measuring administrative burdens stemming from new regulations is increasingly becoming a standard part of the *ex ante* impact assessment process.

Far from being exhaustive, the review of initiatives for evidence-based decision-making outlined in this section especially focuses on the synergies with other efforts to simplify the administrative regime in Latvia and reduce burdens.

The regulatory impact assessment system

In Latvia, the obligation to conduct a regulatory impact assessment (RIA) and the necessary arrangements for the underlying system are set out in a Cabinet Instruction of December 2009.[28] That legal base includes the methodology of quantifying and monetising administrative costs. Such an assessment is to be carried out in cases in which the draft legal act has negative administrative impacts. The instruction defines "administrative costs" as those costs that result from information obligation provision or storing duties.

The Cabinet of Ministers adopted amendments to Instruction No. 19 in June 2017, which entered into force as of 1 January 2018.[29] They provide for a series of new assessments to be conducted as a part of the RIA, including expected impact on small and medium-sized enterprises (SMEs), micro enterprises and start-ups. Moreover, the analysis of impacts on the environment, competition, health and non-governmental organisations (NGOs) will have to be included in the initial impact assessment, together with statements on the compliance requirements. If a new public service is created or redesigned, the RIA must include an analysis of delivery channels and an assessment of the impact on existing or future information and communication technology (ICT) systems.

These and other amendments will be added to a revised version of the existing Handbook on Draft Legislative Act Initial Impact Assessment, elaborated by the State Chancellery.[30] The handbook is complemented by a Guide on Enhanced Standard Cost Model. Furthermore, specific training for policy officials on the new RIA requirements is envisaged by the end of 2017.

To consolidate all necessary information on the RIA system for government initiatives, the State Chancellery published a dedicated section of the electronic Guidebook on Drafting Legislative Acts, which includes downloadable forms and the relevant guidance materials.[31]

Ex post *reviews of regulatory stock*

Similar to several OECD countries, no systemic programme is in place in Latvia on *ex post* reviews of existing regulations. Reviews of regulations are part of the development planning system, and should in principle be conducted as a part of the regulatory process. However, to date such evaluations have tended to be carried out on an ad hoc basis or in particular areas or for particular types of legal acts, for example, with the aim of identifying obsolete legal provisions. Setting up inter-institutional working groups for such reviews is a regular practice.

Further, also to the recognition within the *Saeima* of the need for more systematic evaluation of the implementation of laws, the Cabinet of Ministers adopted a Conceptual Report on “Implementation of *Ex Post* Evaluation” in August 2016,[32] with the aim to improve the oversight of efficient implementation of regulations. Implementing that commitment, the State Chancellery conducted two pilot projects throughout 2017 in co-operation with the *Saeima* and relevant line ministries – namely an *ex post* evaluation of the Law on Volunteers Work and one of the Regulation on Public Administration Employees Performance Evaluation System. On the basis of that experience, the Chancellery will elaborate a methodology for post-implementation regulatory reviews in 2018.

The Digital Agenda and e-Government Strategy

The Digital Agenda and e-Government Strategy are traditionally powerful drivers for administrative simplification in Latvia. Over the years, efforts were made at the central level to develop and mainstream ICT in the public administration, not least through the transposition of European Union legislation in the field.

The current National e-Government Strategy[33] dates back to early 2013, when the Cabinet of Ministers approved a Concept of the Organisational Model of Public ICT Management, on the basis of which the government framed public ICT strategies, principles and scenarios for the effective co-ordination of the public ICT’s development and maintenance through partly centralised and partly sectoral management.

The Cabinet's Information Society Development Guidelines for 2014-2020 of October 2013 were elaborated to ensure continuity of policies in the previous strategic period and to determine the ICT priorities for the EU Structural Funds Programming period until 2020.

At present, the e-government landscape nonetheless remains relatively heterogeneous, with different initiatives managed by, and targeting, various actors within the state administration. Some providers of public services are not directly bound by the government agenda for statutory or budgetary grounds. As a result, the Ministry of Environmental Protection and Regional Development deploys both soft and harder approaches to advance the digitalisation of public administration, relying on high-level political dialogue, memoranda of understanding, as well as more binding Cabinet resolutions. Particular attention is currently put on ensuring a smooth, paperless co-ordination, sharing data across the public administration, and better data management systems. Initiatives related to the one-stop shops, the provision of services and the deployment of e-signature are also part and parcel of the e-government strategies (see Chapter 2). A series of co-operative agreements are also signed with relevant NGOs on matters such as the development of digital skills; Latvia's e-Index; and digital transformation.[34]

Towards a simplified, business-friendlier administration: Governance implications for Latvia

An effective agenda for administrative simplification with untapped potential

Overall, Latvia appears to be on a good reform track, reflecting a strong political commitment to rendering the economy more competitive.

Latvia is developing and advancing many reforms to develop a sound business climate, including pursuing administrative simplification and digitalisation; reviewing its legal framework for commercial activities; and increasing businesses' accessibility to public services, especially through digital means.

While this is also partly the result of complying with EU legislation and policies, it is undeniable that the government set the explicit goal of matching the top world performers in terms of facilitating doing business and stimulating entrepreneurship. The inclusion of targets related to improvement in Latvia's ranking according to established OECD and other international indicators (e.g. World Bank's Doing Business) in government decisions confirms such commitment and increases accountability, while at the same time allowing the government to sustain its reform momentum over time and across several areas of intervention.

Progress is acknowledged and there is general appreciation by private sector stakeholders of the government's work on easing doing business in the country. Both the substance and means to achieve such progress are an asset.

Most of the non-governmental stakeholders met by the OECD (among whom there were representatives of business, trade and professional associations as well as individual entrepreneurs) held a favourable opinion of the progress made by the government in simplifying business procedures and stimulating paperless interactions with the public administration. The sustained and constructive dialogue nurtured by the government with the business community regarding inputs and co-design reforms was also particularly appreciated. The positive climate for reform is confirmed by the acknowledgement of the government of the generally constructive and responsible attitude taken by business in collaborating on the reform programme – an attitude which in turn has encouraged responsiveness and commitment to institutional learning.

There are, in other words, very good framework conditions in place for further reform actions in Latvia. Both the reformers within the public administration and among the reform beneficiaries enjoy a high level of credibility and trust. The approach to reforms also appears to be seen as an asset. With regard to administrative simplification measures at least, it is consensual and participatory, where the responsibilities of all parties involved in the reform endeavour are recognised and leveraged. In this respect, the lack of systematic quantification and measurement efforts by the government to guide the direction of the simplification initiative does not seem to be considered negatively by either party.

Despite the fact that the project itself is still in its early stages of implementation, the approach taken to elaborating the "Consult First" project may be considered the epitome of the Latvian model to reform. It well illustrates the willingness between several actors to enter into constructive dialogue; to listen to the challenges and the constraints faced by both regulators and the regulated; to share good practices and leverage ideas; and to seek a comprehensive scope of application of the innovative solution reached.

The scope of the reforms appears to be quite wide and comprehensive, although challenges remain in relation to the strategic co-ordination, monitoring, accountability and communication of the reform.

As highlighted above, the remit of measures undertaken to simplify and digitalise the public administration encompasses most of the typical areas covered by regulatory policies in OECD countries. Also in terms of ensuring an evidence-based regulatory process, arrangements and guidance are in place that reflect international standards. More generally, regulatory policy elements are embedded in the government's strategic documents and rules of procedure.

Nonetheless, no single, formal, whole-of-government document spells out the regulatory policy of the government. This may hamper the overall effectiveness of the Latvian better regulation agenda, if it prevents the elaboration and implementation of a strategic vision of the reforms. Such a risk may emerge also in light of the relatively dispersed allocation of responsibilities for individual parts of the regulatory reform. In the case of administrative simplification, for instance, leadership, design and management of parallel reform dossiers are spread between the State Chancellery, the Ministry of Justice, the Ministry of Economics, and the Ministry of Environmental Protection and Regional Development, as a minimum.

The lack of standing, institutionalised mechanisms for co-ordination is coupled with a relatively soft power that those ministries can deploy to ensure compliance with the reform targets and deadlines across the state administration. Political discussion at ministerial level must often compensate for failing to formally enforce reform programmes. While it allows for a less hierarchical and potentially more co-operative attitude towards administrative simplification, this approach may not prove the quickest and most effective approach to delivering change.

A further consequence that appears to result from the lack of a centralised policy and a more cohesive leadership to the reform is the rather weak accountability that line ministries appear to enjoy when implementing administrative simplification programmes. To date, neither a regulatory policy in general, or individual reform initiatives in particular, are systematically evaluated in terms of performance against the agreed pace and scope of the reforms. Communication of such progress to the public is also not regular or comprehensive.

Notes

[1] Adopted on 20 November 1990.

[2] Adopted on 22 October 2015

[3] Adopted on 31 October 2002.

[4] Adopted on 10 May 1897.

[5] Adopted on 15 December 1992.

[6] Adopted on 14 October 1998.

[7] Adopted on 21 April 2005.

[8] Adopted on 25 October 2001.

[9] Approved by the CoM Protocol No. 64, Paragraph 57, on 16 November 2010.

[10] See "Strengthening the national economy", Task 34.1 of the Declaration on the implementation of intended activities of the CoM headed by Māris Kučinskis (approved by Decree No. 275 of 3 May 2016).

[11] See www.vraa.gov.lv/en/about_us/

[12] Refer to the OECD Guidelines on Corporate Governance of State-Owned Enterprises (2015 edition), Recommendation II.A (p. 18): "Governments should simplify and standardise the legal forms under which SOEs operate. Their operational practices should follow commonly accepted corporate norms"; the annotation on p. 34 adds: "When standardising the legal form of SOEs, governments should base themselves as much as possible on corporate law that is equally applicable to privately owned companies and avoid creating a specific legal form, or granting SOEs a privileged status or special protection, when this is not absolutely necessary for achieving the public policy objectives imposed on the enterprise."

[13] For further information on the corporate governance of the Hamburg harbour – organised as a listed public company, see https://hhla.de/en/investor-relations/corporate-governance/overview.html.

[14] Although in their tasks they perform equivalent functions as sworn notaries (for instance certifying signatures of natural persons), state notaries are not sworn notaries. State notaries are public officials and their activities are regulated by the State Civil Service Law. They perform the functions specified in the regulatory enactments regulating the scope of the Register of Enterprises. Sworn notaries, by contrast, are officers belonging to the court system and may operate commercially. Their functions are laid down in the Law on the Notaries. Both sworn notaries and state notaries can certify signatures of natural persons on documents that must be submitted to the Enterprise Registry.

[15] While sworn notaries have to follow the Commercial Law, the Notariate Law and the Prevention of Anti-Money Laundering Law, officials of the Enterprise Registry only have to comply with the Commercial Law.

[16] Including verifications in the National Register of persons wanted by the police or in national and international sanction lists.

[17] For example, in Registry of Invalid documents.

[18] Sworn notaries suggested moving the focus from the formal involvement of notaries towards checking the content of notarised statements provided to the Enterprise Registry and share transfer, especially in light of anti-money-laundering policies.

[19] See the Action Plan for Improvement of the Business Environment, February 2017, p. 4.

[20] See also www.mazaksslogs.gov.lv. The State Chancellery administers a related mobile phone application, called *Football*, with the same objectives of receiving complaints about excessive bureaucracy and ideas for its streamlining.

[21] Such development forms part of the Draft Open Government Partnership National Action Plan 2017–2019 and the Draft Public Administration Reform Plan 2020, under the direction of "Moving Towards Zero Bureaucracy".

[22] As of September 2017; draft available at http://tap.mk.gov.lv/doc/2017_07/MKPl_240717_VPRP2020.803.pdf.

[23] See the Draft Public Administration Plan 2020, p. 12.

[24] The specific guidance is OECD (2014), *Regulatory Enforcement and Inspections*, OECD Publishing, Paris, http://dx.doi.org/10.1787/9789264208117-en.

[25] Among them are the largest Latvian enforcement authorities, including the State Revenue Service; the State Environmental Service; the Consumer Rights Protection Centre; the Insolvency Administration; the State Agency of Medicines; the Nature Conservation Agency; and the Cross-sector Coordination Centre.

[26] Six modules are foreseen under the project, covering issues related to the regulatory environment; less regulation and administrative burden reduction; communication with entrepreneurs and monitoring and enforcement; public service delivery; competition; and sustainable entrepreneurship.

[27] The portal, which will be located at www.gov.lv, will serve as a web platform for both state and municipal institutions.

[28] See Cabinet Instruction No. 19 on Rules for Completing the Initial Impact Assessment of a Draft Legal Act, available at https://likumi.lv/doc.php?id=203061.

[29] The related Cabinet Instruction 4/2017 is available at http://tap.mk.gov.lv/doc/2017_06/MKinstr_07042017_Anot_groz.1253.docx.

[30] The two sets of methodological and analytical guidelines mentioned can be found at www.mk.gov.lv/sites/default/files/editor/metodika_gala1.pdf and www.mk.gov.lv/sites/default/files/editor/3_1_as_metrgr_psim_e-vide1_final.pdf

[31] See https://tai.mk.gov.lv/anotacija.

[32] See http://polsis.mk.gov.lv/documents/5677.

[33] See http://www.varam.gov.lv/eng/darbibas_ve-IDi/e_gov/?doc=13317.

[34] The related Cooperation Memoranda with NGOs can be found at www.varam.gov.lv/lat/lidzd/Sad_nvo/?doc=14926.

References

Business Regulation (n.d.), "Making it Easier for Business", www.businessregulation.ie/ (accessed 11 May 2018).

Cunningham, N. and Sinclair, D. (1999), 'Regulatory Pluralism: Designing Policy Mixes for Environmental Protection', Blackwell Publishers Ltd, Law & Policy, Vol. 21, No. 1, January 1999.

Government of Latvia (2012), "National Development Plan of Latvia for 2014–2020", Cross-Sectoral Coordination Centre (CCSC), www.pkc.gov.lv/images/NAP2020%20dokumenti/NDP2020_English_Final.pdf.

International Finance Corporation (2016), "Making Mediation Law", *Mediation Series*, http://documents.worldbank.org/curated/en/899611503551941578/pdf/119067-WP-REV-11-9-2017-15-33-48-MakingMedLaw.pdf.

Ireland – Department of Business, Enterprise and Innovation, website, Business Regulation, "Making it Easier for Business", www.businessregulation.ie/ (accessed 11 May 2018).

Latvia - Cross-Sectoral Coordination Centre, website, https://www.pkc.gov.lv/en/about-us (accessed 23 April 2018).

Latvia - Ministry of Economy (2016), "The impact of administrative procedures on business environment".

OECD (2017), Corporate Governance in Latvia, OECD Publishing, Paris, http://dx.doi.org/10.1787/9789264268180-en.

OECD (2016), "Latvia", in The Governance of Inclusive Growth: An Overview of Country Initiatives, OECD Publishing, Paris, http://dx.doi.org/10.1787/9789264265189-25-en.

OECD (2014), Regulatory Enforcement and Inspections, OECD Publishing, Paris, http://dx.doi.org/10.1787/9789264208117-en.

OECD (2010), Better Regulation in Europe: Portugal 2010, OECD Publishing, Paris, http://dx.doi.org/10.1787/9789264084575-en.

UK - gov.uk (n.d.), "Business and self-employed", webpage, www.gov.uk/browse/business (accessed 11 May 2018).

Chapter 3. Centring service infrastructure on business needs in Latvia: a continuum of public services for businesses

This chapter examines the accessibility of services for businesses presenting a concept of a continuum of legal and justice services. In line with the OECD Serving Citizen framework it focuses on services provided by the state (Enterprise Registry, State Land service and Registry and the Patent Office). The chapter puts a particular emphasis on digital tools and provides an overview of e-services available for businesses in Latvia. This chapter also identifies the characteristics and impact of legal problems experienced by Latvian businesses.

Towards a user-centred holistic approach

There is growing understanding that the accessibility of services plays a key role in a complex service system that consists of many institutions and actors, and that the system needs to be addressed as a whole. Service provision systems must be understood as a series of pathways for receiving services from the perspective of individuals, businesses and communities. In the course of their lifecycle, small, medium and large companies engage with multiple public services to register their activities, apply for licences, file business income and reporting, hire employees, resolve a dispute, etc. Public services for business are often fragmented across different administrations. Businesses, and particularly small and medium-sized enterprises (SMEs) who do not have the capability or resources (human, financial - or time), may feel overwhelmed (Pleasence and Balmer, 2013).

The OECD Serving Citizens Framework underlines that governmental responsibility to provide a wide range of public services should be designed to meet the expectations and needs of their citizens in terms of access, responsiveness and reliability/quality. Since legal and justice services are considered as public services, affordability of legal procedures as well as access to legal information are key in assessing the degree of accessibility of the judicial system. Service delivery reflects citizens' perceptions of public institutions: satisfaction with services as well as with public institutions and governments (OECD, 2015a).

Some OECD countries are integrating a business-centred approach to the provision of services. This dynamic service planning tool is developed around the "life events" of businesses. This helps organise public service delivery to meet the specific needs of their constituencies as well as assess the outcome of the service based on the experience of users (European Commission, 2015). Some countries (e.g. Colombia, Tunisia) are integrating (representatives of) courts and tribunals into multi-service centres in order to enhance the delivery of justice services and make those institutions accessible to, and reflective of, users' needs.

In Latvia, the Ministry of Justice supervises key justice services related to the business life cycle including the following independent state institutions: the Enterprise Registry, State Land Service and the Patent Office (Figure 3.1). They are the focus of this chapter.

Figure 3.1. Institutions subordinated to the Ministry of Justice in Latvia

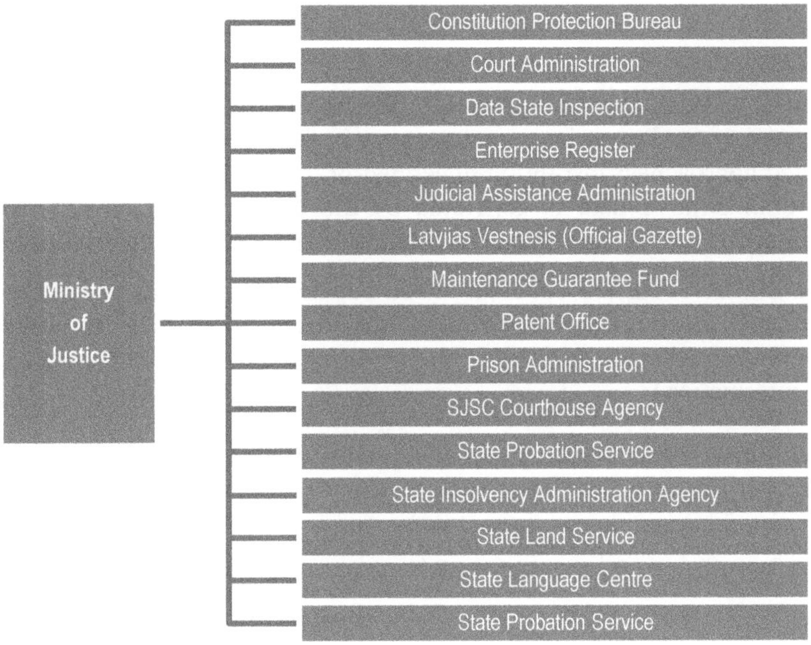

Source: Latvia – Ministry of Justice website.

Businesses in Latvia also have to register as a Value-Added Tax (VAT) payer at the State Revenue Service (SRS). The Latvian Central Depository (LCD), a privately owned institution, is the sole central publicly traded securities depository, maintaining the securities recording and settlement in Latvia. Supervised by the Financial and Capital Markets Commission, LCD further provides transaction services. For such private entities, the regulatory challenge is to respect their entrepreneurial character while at the same time ensuring the provision of public services. Beyond the existing institutions and entities, incentives might be considered for further private services to add to the basic functions of state business services.

A multi-level approach to understanding business needs

Business engagement

A strong consultation culture exists in Latvia that needs to fully encompass the views of all businesses. The Action Plans as well as other legal and regulatory reforms related to the business activities are developed in collaboration with various organisations representing businesses, including the Foreign Investors Council in Latvia, the Latvian Chamber of Commerce and Industry, and the Employers' Confederation of Latvia. Yet according to Ministry of Economy's survey on the impact of administrative procedures on the business environment, while the level of engagement has grown since 2014, it remains weak: 75% of entrepreneurs, mainly small businesses, do not participate in any industry/business association or union (71% of large companies engage in business-to-government [B2G] discussions; 57% of medium-sized companies; and 30% of small companies). Reasons cited include the lack of reason to participate (54% of respondents), lack of time (23% of respondents) and the absence of sufficient information (18.6% of respondents) are mainly cited. Importantly, this consultation needs to also take place with non-business stakeholders, e.g. consumer groups, trade unions.

Business needs

The starting point is to identify the needs, i.e. capture the legal needs of users and understand their pathways and experience and the gaps in the provision of services. There are two inter-related approaches: institution-generated or "administrative" data and legal needs surveys. Administrative data is generated by the different service providers in Latvia. Client satisfaction surveys are also conducted in some of the targeted services.

As part of this report, Latvia carried out a survey on business legal needs and experience to understand the good practices and bottlenecks from the point of view of businesses when accessing services under the purview of the Ministry of Justice (see Figure 3.2 and below for further information).

Figure 3.2. Business legal needs: Types and number of businesses surveyed

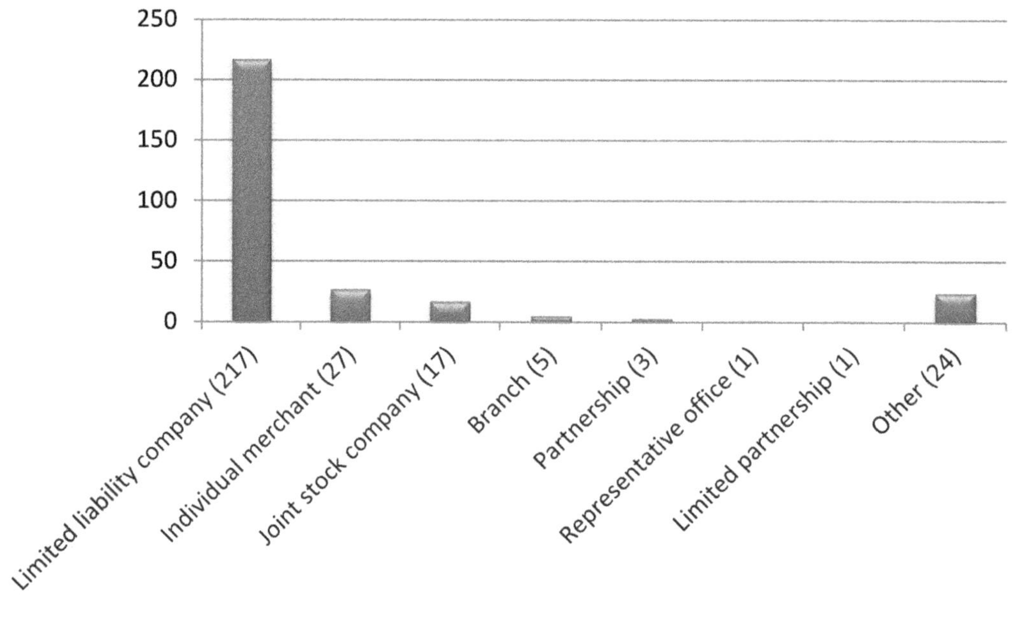

Source: OECD (2017a)

An operational public service environment for businesses

A one-stop shop for citizens and businesses

Creating an efficient and comprehensive entry point for citizens and businesses to access the public administration and enjoy services is a further priority of the Latvian government, as in many other OECD countries (see Box 3.1 for an example). While one-stop-shop services are recognised as a central characteristic of public services for businesses, their implementation remains a challenge. One-stop shop refers to services that are bundled at one central access point. The perspective for one-stop-shop services is that of the users, not necessarily that of the providers. In Korea, one-stop shops operate for all civil application services provided by all Korean administrative bodies, at national and local levels (OECD, 2003). The Mexican government, with the support of the OECD created the one-stop shop tuempresa.gob.mx to simplify the federal procedures required to create a business entity and to help entrepreneurs fulfil these procedures on line (OECD, 2009). Greece and Hungary have specialised in one-stop shops for foreign investors (OECD, 2003).

Box 3.1. Austria's business service portal

In 2010, the Austrian federal government launched a one-stop business service portal (*Unternehmensserviceportal* –USP). It is a centralised online portal for businesses that provides comprehensive information for entrepreneurs and offers direct access to a number of e-government services. The portal serves as a single entry point for businesses and aims to create a favourable environment for setting up and running a business in Austria.

Upon registration, businesses have access to several features, such as:

- a virtual tax office (*FinanzOnline*)
- social insurance services (Electronic Data Exchange of Social Insurance)
- a data-processing register
- e-invoicing to the federal government
- lobbying and Advocacy Register
- a transparency database (publications of information about subsidies and transfers).

Moreover, the USP offers regular updates, information and tips regarding regulatory aspects of commercial activities, e.g. concerning personnel; tax; starting a business; searching for forms; or searching for the competent authority.

Source: Austria - Unternehmensserviceportal.

Since 2015 Latvia has continued to update its one-stop-shop approach to group procedures from the State Land Service and the Land Registry offices.[1] Public services that could be considered to form part of a broader one-stop-shop approach for businesses are, for example: the Enterprise Registry, the State Land Service, Land Registry offices (which are under court jurisdiction), the Patent Office, the business arm of the Tax Authority and relevant licencing authorities.

In Latvia, a Public Administration Service Portal (www.latvija.lv) is operational, the remit of which is progressively expanding to include an increasing number of e-services. Managed by the State Regional Development Agency, the portal is the visible part of a developed national shared services platform. It consists of three levels: information, consultation and e-procedures (from basic e-documents sent by email to advanced, fully automated e-services). The portal also provides the opportunity to carry out e-services payments. As such, the portal serves as the Latvian "Point of Single Contact" for services, as provided for by EU legislation. The availability of e-services is provided also through the institutions' websites. At present, more than 500 e-services are made available to citizens and businesses, mainly through the Public Administration Service Portal. In the case of the State Revenue Service, all formalities must now take place directly on line.

The Ministry of Environmental Protection and Regional Development is currently re-designing its underlying concept in order to make the portal more user-friendly and, ultimately, make the interface with the public smoother and more effective, as called for by some stakeholders.

In parallel, the Ministry of Economy started a new initiative to create a one-stop-shop website for businesses in Latvia. An improved one-stop portal is in the planning process and funds are already allocated. Some technological progress is already implemented to centralise such services.

In order to be truly effective, a one-stop shop should be designed strictly from the perspective of the users – rather than from the providers'. Users should not be concerned with differentiating between the competences of state agencies or have to engage in identifying and coping with the relevant legal provisions. They should, however, be required to provide a certain piece of information only once. This applies in particular, if such information is relevant for a higher number of state agencies. For example, even though the identity and address of the directors of a company are relevant for the Enterprise Registry, Land Registry offices and the Tax Authority, a one-stop shop approach requires this information only once. This would apply even if the different authorities require the information at different times. Currently, the users of public services are to provide the same piece of information multiple times when dealing with different state agencies. Reducing this to one-off submission only yields both private and public cost savings. Businesses would lower their registration costs and agencies would save costs since the information processing at the front end only happens once – instead of multiple times. This would have the added benefit of all services working on the basis of a consistent and identical data set. The current uncoordinated multiple requests of information by multiple public administrative bodies carry the risk of incoherent decisions and unpredictability. Some stakeholders have complained about such decisions being based on conflicting data.

The potential of one-stop-shop services is driven by information technology (IT) where electronic solutions are at the core of the one-stop-shop strategy (see below). Websites and data platforms facilitate centralised public services using data economies of scale in an unprecedented way. Consequently, such initiatives should aim to reduce the need for users to physically come to state agencies. This might be achieved by physically bringing the contact points for business-related services into one building or closer together. Stakeholders reported that – at present – the offices of public services are usually spread over different locations across the country, e.g. Enterprise Registry. Occasionally stakeholders also mentioned that they still want to be able to interact face to face with service staff. A compromise solution could be to allow for video communication where businesses arrange for an e-meeting and discuss with a service provider over video.

Provision of e-services

Beyond one-stop shops, the provision of e-services is a fundamental element to streamline administrative procedures for the everyday life of each citizen. It is, at the same time, an integral part of the commitment by the European Union to create a digital single market that minimises administrative burdens for economic operators. From 1 September 2018 all EU citizens should be able to receive cross-border electronic services through a qualified identification and identification tool provided in each member state. In Portugal, the Simplex/Simplex+ (administrative and legislative simplification programme) project aimed at fostering a better business environment, improving citizens' lives and reducing costs for the Portuguese administration. This programme was based on cross-department and multi-level collaboration, and joined e-government and cutting-red-tapes initiatives (OECD, 2010a).[2]

The Government of Latvia is actively engaged in securing the elaboration and circulation of e-documents between individuals and institutions as well as the provision of e-services to end users. Every natural and legal person in Latvia has the right to use e-documents to communicate with all state and local government institutions as well as courts and public service providers. Such communication may take place either on line through the Public Administration Service Portal or through consumer service centres across the country. As mentioned, the State Regional Development Agency is thus developing a unified technical solution (e.g. memorandum of understanding at ministerial level as regards data protocols; see below) that will provide these tasks and will be integrated into the Public Administration Service Portal. In addition, providing the services (e.g. forms) in English and other languages could also help develop an international, business-friendly environment.

The Law on "Official Electronic Address" took effect on 1 March 2018, which provides for a legal framework to facilitate the circulation of e-documents and the more efficient use and development of e-services. A single electronic environment linked to a specific e-address will be created, to which each user will receive and store all their correspondence with public institutions, regardless of the authority and the matter at hand. The law also provides that an email account will only be accessible through qualified personal electronic identification means.

The Estonian experience shows some positive outcomes following the automation of most public sector processes (e-Governance Academy (n.d.)): more than 80% of Estonian enterprises now communicate with the public sector using e-channels; the duration of a business-starting process went from five days to two hours; public information (tax, commercial, procurement issues) about companies is now easily accessible and usable, which is deemed to have a direct impact on preventing money laundering and corruption.

Box 3.2. Estonia's e-residency model

E-residency of Estonia is a programme launched by Estonia in 2014 and opened to location-independent entrepreneurs from all over the world. E-residents receive a government-issued digital ID card that enables them to access Estonian public and private sector e-services and resources. E-residency provides the ability to remotely take the following actions:

- digitally sign documents and contracts
- verify the authenticity of signed documents
- encrypt and transmit documents securely
- establish an Estonian company on line
- administer your company from anywhere in the world
- apply for third-party services like e-banking and remote money transfers
- access online payment service providers
- declare Estonian taxes on line.

To date, 27 068 applications were submitted from 143 countries. Using digital ID card and e-services, 4 273 companies were established in Estonia.

Source: Estonia - E-residency website.

Prompted by the risk of fraud via e-services, certain Latvian stakeholders (other than the sworn notaries) thought that this was a theoretical risk only. According to them, e-services could be safer than physical checks as it will be easier to optimise multiple checks. Currently sworn notaries only conduct limited checks (see below). An e-residency approach in Latvia such as in Estonia might be helpful, in particular, to improve investment opportunities for foreigners in Latvia by decreasing the time and costs necessary for registering business participation.

Discussing e-services with business stakeholders, it was revealed that many do not know enough about e-services and, as a consequence, do not use them. Also, not all agencies apply e-signatures at this point in time (see below). Finally coverage of fast optical fibre cable-based internet across the territory could be necessary for the take up of e-services in all regions of Latvia.

Leveraging information and communication technology (ICT) at the front and back ends

The use of IT mainly concerns two essential dimensions: the front end presented to users and the back end that deals with data management and decision making. Both dimensions matter equally and both dimensions offer enormous potential for cost reductions. In fact, it is only if both dimensions and additionally their inter-relationship is perfected that the potential of IT in public services is fully employed. To give just one example, improvements in data management and decision making at the back end will only develop their full potential if communicated in a user-centric way, such that businesses minimise their costs.

According to stakeholders, the business community is eager to see IT solutions uphold high-quality standards for the prevention of fraud. The majority of consulted stakeholders see an electronic public services approach as a chance to detect fraud. The thought was that data analytics could be used to detect fraud patterns in a way that mere identity checking would not discover.

The front end: Electronic identification, e-certification and e-empowerment

Security and reliability in working in an electronic environment require the issuance of individual e-identities to verify personal identification and allow personalised e-services. The Public Administration Service Portal identifies individuals for different services using various identification methods with different legal bases, security levels and usability. Common types of identity certification (authentication) in Latvia are:

- **Authentication systems maintained by the institutions**: In order to authenticate their customers, the institutions create a specific authentication solution in their information systems, usually granting the user a username and password.
- **Authentication by Internet banking**: By integrating the Internet banking mechanism into their information systems, institutions can allow identified individual users access to the relevant services and information. This authentication type depends on the voluntary agreement by the bank to such co-ordination, which cannot be guaranteed by the institutions, so might not be effective in the long run.
- **Mobile ID**: Users can certify their identity remotely by using a mobile phone. Mobile ID is incorporated in the phone SIM card and merely requires mobile network coverage.
- **Electronic identification (e-ID) cards**: The government committed to making the e-ID card a free, mandatory document for residents in Latvia, providing for a transitional period from 2019 to 2022.[3] The e-ID card contains biometric data and information in electronic form to enable both the electronic verification of the holder's identity and the creation of a secure e-signature. As such, the e-ID card can serve both as an identity and travel document within the EU and as the most secure personal identification tool for accessing e-services.
- **Authentication by e-signature**: This solution relies on an e-signature identification smart card. This authentication mode allows individuals to sign documents electronically and to access a variety of online e-services. Currently in Latvia three safe electronic signature types are available – virtual e-signatures (*eParaksts*), e-signatures on smart cards and e-signatures on e-IDs. While stakeholders mentioned that not all agencies accept e-signatures in their correspondence, the possibilities to make use of e-signatures are expanding in Latvia. As a rule, all state and municipal authorities are now obliged to accept electronic documents signed with a qualified e-signature. The timestamp is used along with e-signature in communications with state or local government institutions. The timestamp records electronically and thus bears proof of the time a document is signed. Currently the stakeholders have to pay for their e-signatures if they exceed a forfeit free use threshold; from 2019 it will be completely free and mandatory. It is hoped that the general availability of e-signatures will further support their use in practice. According to the experience in Estonia, mandatory e-signatures could increase the uptake of e-services.

The diffusion and use of certain e-identification means are disparate in Latvia. For instance holders of the Latvian e-ID card may, moreover, enjoy a forfeit of 120 individual free uses of e-signatures during the validity period of the card, after which the service unfolds on a pay-per-use basis. Technical challenges have also been identified, which tend to complicate or even prevent the authentication on the user's website. The government recognises such hurdles.[4] This considerably limits the attractiveness and effectiveness of the card, thereby hampering the legal certainty and trust in the e-ID card as a single and personally available universal means of identification.

Moreover the framework regulating the use of various means of identification is not uniform, and access to e-services is not evenly guaranteed in Latvia. The use of an identification tool is currently subject to an agreement between the provider of the service, the one of the identity identification, and the recipient of the service. Alternatively, separate provisions are needed in the legislation governing the specific public service.

Looking ahead, e-signatures alone are not the ultimate IT solution to businesses services. E-platform solutions offer more attractive cost-benefit relations than mere e-signature approaches. The essential reason is that e-platform solutions allow users to enter their data directly on the website and the entries are automatically transferred to the database. Using e-signature only approaches where, for example, the e-signature is attached to a PDF document, usually still requires someone to transfer the data from the document to the database. Hence, platform services offer greater cost savings.

Implementing e-services and promoting the use of e-identification in Latvia and other countries would need to take into account a population that is less tech-savvy and knowledgeable or have limited access to the Internet. It is thus important that going forward Latvia ensure e-empowerment. Stakeholder discussions emphasised that a considerable number of users were either not aware of already existing e-solutions or were equipped with wrong or outdated information on such possibilities. This highlights the need for information initiatives and getting support from core actors.

The back end: Common data management and protocol

With regard to the back end, stakeholders recommended a common data management covering all public services. In particular, establishing a common data protocol and common data standards/interfaces for all public services is key to the one-stop-shop approach, cost efficiency and facilitating the provision of e-services. While probably no one would dispute the usefulness of common data protocols and interfaces, they are sometimes difficult to achieve in practice. Different agencies might insist on their specific protocols and require exceptions, or co-operate half-heartedly. It seems necessary to establish an institutional and procedural framework that ensures the full participation of all service providers.

One solution is to set up a central body with the responsibility for harmonising data protocols and monitoring whether development milestones are met in a timely fashion. In Latvia this approach could build on the initiative from the Ministry of Environment and Regional Development. A memorandum of understanding at ministerial level is being developed that is intended to facilitate the harmonisation and quality of data protocols.

In terms of technical details, the Estonian e-residency model and the use of the Estonian open platform service, which is available as open source might be considered (see above; Box 3.2). The X-road project, which serves as the backbone of e-Estonia allows for "data exchange in a secure, decentralised, low-cost manner". Some 600 information systems from the public and private sectors are linked in the state information administration system, together with more than 3 000 services.

Figure 3.3. Estonia's X-Road project for secure and decentralised data exchange

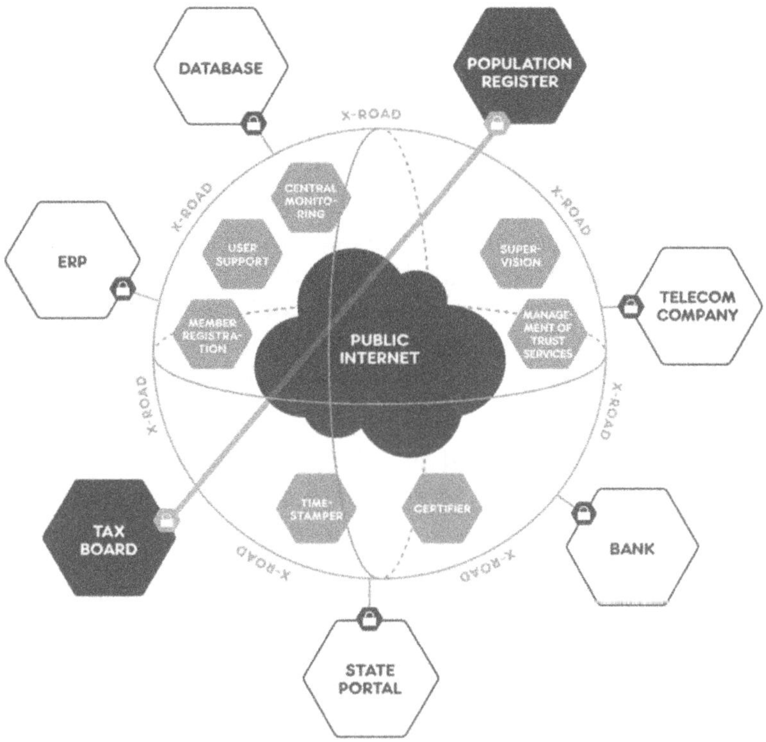

Source: Estonia - Business Register (2017).

As mentioned for the design of the one-stop-shop website, the IT solutions should – from the start – be designed with foreign users in mind. This concerns back-end issues, such as the intake of data and the verification of information.

Moving forward: Investing in ever more efficient procedures for economic activities

Overall, although the government seems to have identified the reform fronts that require further action, and many of the issues raised by the stakeholders are already included in future reforms measures, a number of pending challenges persist, specifically in relation to the three formalities investigated below – i.e. the application procedures for registration and the re-organisation of businesses:

- **Digital signature and online services**: While entrepreneurs' awareness of e-signature services is reported to be on the rise, its level of use does not reflect its potential benefits. This is partly due to the still widespread perception among the public that printed documents are legally more secure and binding than electronic files. A certain distrust in e-government is still embedded culturally in Latvia, although the main obstacles for a swifter diffusion of it are due to the lack of financial resources to set up the necessary e-infrastructure and the generally insufficient literacy and skills related to dealing with digital procedures and e-documents. Further reasons include the difficulty in implementation (78% of non-users) or the lack of information about the service (70% of non-users); the limited number of services accepting e-signatures; and mixed registration processes whereby not all documents can be submitted on line.

In addition, it currently seems difficult to use all services consistently on line. For example, notary certificates generally require personal attendance. It needs to be considered which functions really require personal attendance and where online-only services might be possible. Stakeholders reported that only small and simple companies could be registered on line, while larger and more complex registrations were not possible online-only (for example, if VAT is involved). One solution is to make use of the Estonian open platform service, which is available as open source. In addition, initiatives should keep in mind to incentivise private services to complement the basic functions of state business services. It could also be useful if e-services are organised by lifecycle; not so many companies use e-services (about 30%) so the issues are more about the mentality, although e-service take-up is higher for younger generations.

Other general challenges identified are, first, the setting up of a common data management covering all public services and an associated state institution and, second, the implementation of the ambitious plans to create a one-stop shop and easy-to-use public services. Tools that might support the process of setting up a working e-ecosystem and e-ID-system might be considered, for example an institution taking care of the harmonisation of data protocols and monitoring development milestones. Generally, it was suggested that e-platform solutions should be considered to go beyond e-signature approaches. This is because e-platform entries can be directly fed into the data system, while e-signature approaches still require manual data entry at public service level. Currently, entrepreneurs can optionally obtain an e-signature and use it with public services. Foreign e-signatures are currently not accepted, even if European. In addition, stakeholders stressed that agencies should work on the basis of the same information; currently they sometimes use conflicting information. Agencies should also make sure the user does not need to submit data twice, which currently is the case. The government seems to be aware of the disadvantages caused by the current heterogeneous electronic environment in Latvia. In particular, continued reliance on the fragmented, non-transparent framework for the electronic identification of the service recipient prevents citizens and businesses from fully exercising their right to receive state-guaranteed electronic services regardless of location. Individuals are not provided with steadily available and universally applicable means of electronic identification in order to receive an electronic service provided by the state for which the state is responsible for the safety and long-term operation. Economically, moreover, the current system is inefficient and burdensome on the public budget, and obliges commercial entities to invest extra financial resources in the development of new, individualised electronic identification solutions for their e-services.

- **Service costs**: The costs of services were raised as an issue. The fact that negotiated discounted fees are offered to applicants if they opt to follow the digital procedure indicates that the fees are not set at cost-recovery levels. There seems to be scope for internationally comparing the costs of services and adjusting them.
- **Communication and language:** One issue, mentioned several times, is the perception that state services do not communicate among themselves in a way that ensures coherent decisions from the perspective of the users. Central data

management would be a first and important step towards coherent decision making. The perception of coherent decisions, however, does not only depend on the internal process of decision making. In addition, the external communication of processes and guidelines plays an important role in the acceptance of public services by citizens. One way to improve the communication between users and agencies is the publication of easy-to-use and easy-to-access best practice guidelines. Such guidelines can create a common ground between agencies and users and will improve the acceptance of procedures and results.

In addition, users gave thought to the question whether communication with them could be improved. Some felt that the register could maybe resort to quick and easy types of communication in cases where only minor issues in an application were problematic, such as a missing middle name. To address this issue, Latvia is introducing the use of artificial intelligence in the form of a chatbot for customer information and care. Considering the amount of reform and practical changes underway, communicating these initiatives to users will be key. With a view to attracting foreign investors, the register website already contains optional English and Russian languages. However, as of October 2017, these language options are not implemented without exceptions. Already on the first page of the English version, some part of the text is shown in Latvian. Against this background, stakeholders were very pleased to hear that there are ongoing discussions on whether the services should start communicating fully in English.

A final proposal from stakeholders in terms of communication concerns the communication of state services cross-border. Those stakeholders involved in cross-border investment felt that Latvian agencies at times create unnecessary hurdles for investors based in other countries. These hurdles concern the provision of information by foreign investors and the formal requirements for documents from such investors. In particular, foreign investment is hampered by the requirement of physical presence in Latvia for certain procedures. Similarly, unnecessary costs might be created in cases where Latvian law requires a certain legal form – for example a notarised document – when the home jurisdiction of the foreign investors does not provide such a form – many other countries do not have notaries. The experience of stakeholders shows that such complications either increase the costs of foreign investments due to costly attempts to work around or lead to the failure of such foreign investment.

- **Quality discrepancies at the sub-national level**: Beyond the specific procedures considered for the measurement, business representatives pointed to some disproportionate costs imposed on business by various public administrations, notably when it comes to the delivery of public services at the local level (e.g. construction permits) where municipalities appear to still need to embark on major reforms. In those instances, businesses cannot expect the same clarity and predictability of public decisions that are to be found when interacting with several state administrations.

Business-related services under the Ministry of Justice

Enterprise Registry

Commercial registries are key enablers of the business environment and bear important economic relevance (European Commerce Registers Forum, 2016) (Box 3.3). Incorporating a business creates the corporate veil and allows the business to operate and access the financial and justice sectors. Registered companies may bid on public sector contracts. Registries hold information that helps businesses make targeted business decisions based on their sector or geographical location as well as build the confidence of other parties (suppliers or customers) to contract with the registered businesses. Besides tax purposes, such data can be collected for other key official statistics on the country's economic environment (OECD, 2015b).

Box 3.3. The business registration process in OECD countries

OECD countries are developing specific measures to counter informal business environments by providing easier business registration processes.

In Chile, the Tu Empresa en Un Día (Your Company in One Day) programme enabled limited liability companies to register through a free-of-charge online platform, hosted by the Ministry of Economy. The registration process is reduced to filling out an electronic form with information on the company and shareholders. In addition, the online platform is directly linked to the tax agency, which means that taxpayer identification is automatically provided when a business is registered through this means. The programme had an almost immediate impact on the formalisation of businesses in the country and is now used by a majority of companies. According to the programme's latest activity report, 73.6% of the businesses created in May 2017 went through the programme, which means an increase of 12.4% compared to the same month a year earlier.

In Estonia, the e-Business Register programme also had a significant impact on companies willing to start a business in the country. This online platform gathers several governmental services on line (business registration, business information and data, land registry). According to the Information System Authority, this tool allows a business to register a new entity, change existing information in the business register, and file XBRL (eXtensible Business Reporting Language, the standard used to define and exchange business and financial performance information) annual reports. Through the platform, the duration of business registration is deemed to have decreased from five days to two hours.

Brønnøysund Register Centre is a government agency under the Norwegian Ministry of Trade. The agency facilitates electronic business registration. It provides pre-filled electronic forms with information for several public registers, including the Register of Business Enterprises. The platform includes legal checks so the notification of registration is already proofed when submitted, preventing users from completing the requirements and sending documentation back and forth. The centre introduced the electronic signature for all notifications. Such electronic registration constitutes a great majority of all notifications received by the Register of Business Enterprises. This digital solution is user-friendly, enabling companies to easily and quickly update their registered data.

Source: Chile - "Tu Empresa en Un Día" (2017); May; e-Governance Academy (n.d.); Norway - Brønnøysund Register Centre website.

The registry is headed by the Chief State Notary, who is appointed by the Minister of Justice. The Chief State Notary may be dismissed by the Cabinet of Ministers. Similar to 15 other OECD countries (out of 25 surveyed) the government is the primary source of funding for the Enterprise Registry - compared to a customer fees model (Table 3.1.

Funding models of commercial registers in 27 OECD countries and jurisdictions). The Latvian Enterprise Registry joined the European Business Registers Interconnection System (BRIS) in June 2017.[5] Its activities are regulated, among other things, by the Law on the Registry of Enterprises of the Republic of Latvia of 2005 and the Regulations of the Register approved by the Cabinet of Ministers.[6] The Commercial Law further determines the legal events requiring registration, and other laws regulating formal aspects of the registration process, including the Law on Electronic Documents and the Law on the Notaries.

Table 3.1. Funding models of commercial registers in 27 OECD countries and jurisdictions

Government funded	Customer fees
Australia (ASIC)	Canada (federal)
Austria	Denmark
Belgium	Finland
Canada (e.g. Alberta, British Colombia, Quebec, Nova Scotia)	France
Chile	Italy
Czech Republic	Luxembourg
Estonia	New Zealand
Germany	Spain
Ireland	Sweden
Israel	United Kingdom
Latvia	United States (e.g. Colorado, Minnesota, Montana, Nevada, Washington, DC and Washington State)
Netherlands	
Norway	
Portugal	
Slovenia	
Switzerland	
Turkey	
United Kingdom – Isle of Man	
United States (e.g. Connecticut, North Carolina, North Dakota, Texas)	

Source: European Commerce Registers Forum (2016).

Services of Enterprise Registries integrate notaries and banking counter services as well as VAT registration. The Registry employs several state notaries, whose main task is to verify the submitted documents for compliance with legislation; register commercial companies and organisations; and record changes in the basic documents. Additionally, state notaries also certify signatures on the documents that must be submitted to the Enterprise Registry.[7]

Accessing the service in practice

The reality of registration activity is dominated by private limited liability companies. In 2017, private limited liability companies accounted for more than 90% of all entities registered in the Enterprise Registry (ranging from sole traders, general partnerships, limited partnerships and private limited liability companies to public limited liability companies) (Figure 3.4).

Figure 3.4. Types of registered companies in Latvia

Source: Enterprise Registry as of August 2017.

Stakeholders voiced their general satisfaction with and trust in the services provided by the Enterprise Registry.[8] The services provided by the Enterprise Registry are said to be widely used. Out of 96 businesses surveyed, 89 declared having used them in the last 3 months. The services were obtained on line (17); partially on line (18); by email (10) and in person at the Enterprise Registry (20). Entrepreneurs knew where to go and apply or whom to contact, or where they stand in the process. Respondents spoke highly of the staff working in the Registry. Two respondents declared corruption or bribery was involved. Businesses additionally mentioned the following aspects: when accounts are sent to the tax authority, they are forwarded to the register; registration fees are low. While business registration is seen as efficient, businesses reported that time spent to register at the Enterprise Registry increased between 2014 and 2017, from 5.7 to 6.4 days.[9] This increase was greater when it came to registering for VAT status at the State Revenue Service. As in other OECD countries, after registration, businesses have to apply for business licences, which is said to be cumbersome in Latvia. According to their experience, registration is easy and straightforward if it is a single person registration but cumbersome if a more complicated structure or a foreign investor is to be registered.

A number of stakeholders also reported that a number of businesses are registered in Estonia, while conducting their businesses in Latvia. It is difficult to establish the reasons for this perception[10] and this pattern with certainty. Possible reasons for setting up business in Estonia discussed with shareholders are possible reputational advantages of the Estonian legal framework brand, tax arbitrage and the more facilitative culture of the Estonian registers and institutions. Should this trend be confirmed, it is recommended to establish the causes for this pattern, as these would be symptoms of a legal or factual structure that might require regulatory action.

Many factors impact the complexity and timing of the registration process, including the handling and format of submission (paper, web-based/online forms, pdf images); the level of control/legal checks. Paperwork requirements and the complexity of the process were said to be the most unreasonable; the highest rate of replies (29) said it took them between one day and one week to obtain the service from filing to application, albeit the preparation of the paperwork was not found difficult. Legal empowerment of businesses through clearer information could help alleviate the perception of complexity and time waste (Figure 3.5. Main barriers to accessing the services of the Enterprise Registry).

Figure 3.5. Main barriers to accessing the services of the Enterprise Registry

Based on 102 replies from 50 businesses

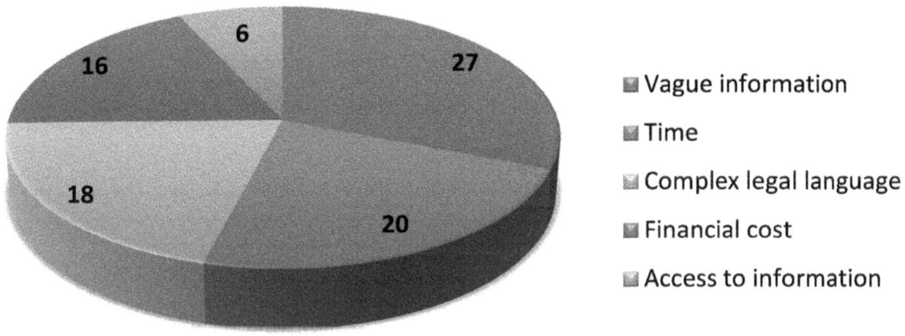

Source: OECD (2017a).

Avenues for service improvement according to surveyed businesses

Stakeholders made a number of suggestions to further simplify and speed up the registration process in specific instances (Figure 3.6). These are presented in the following sections and should be read in light of the cost assessments made in Chapter 3.

Figure 3.6. Main avenues for service improvement of the Enterprise Registry

Based on 162 replies from 50 businesses

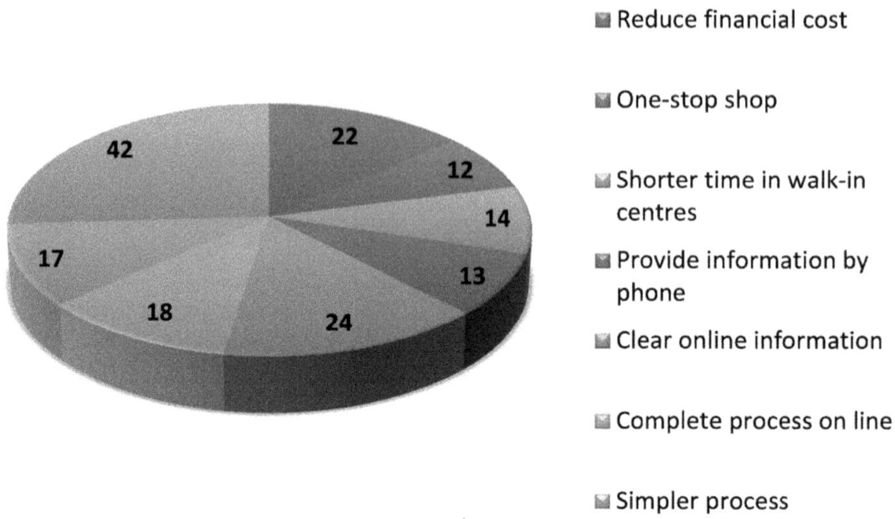

Source: OECD (2017a).

Service fees and financial costs for businesses

The majority of business respondents (out of 50) found the service to be affordable; yet the financial burden was still seen to be heavy (Figure 3.5). Discussions with stakeholders revealed that there is more to the issue of service costs than the reduction of service costs at the back end as a basis for lowering the price of services charged to users. One such further element is the fact that state agencies are in a position to lower service costs to clients beyond transferring their own cost savings. The perspective for discovering such cost savings on the user side is to consider the intermediary position of the state agencies. Whenever the agencies manage to offer their services in a way that maintains their cost level, but reduces the costs on the users' side, an overall cost reduction is achieved.

One example for achieving such cost reductions is to offer standard documents, simple forms and guidelines to spare businesses the need to ask for professional advice. In particular, small and medium-sized businesses for which such advisory costs are relatively higher will benefit from such measures. A further element is to develop a coherent approach to pricing services. Such a coherent approach would consider the effects of service charges on the behaviour of users. For example, prices might be used to nudge users toward the use of e-platform services, which in turn triggers economy of scale advantages in terms of back-end costs, as mentioned above. Further, cross-services price comparisons can be used to understand the reality of pricing from the perspective of the users. Finally, international price comparisons – in particular with closely competing jurisdictions – can reveal information for strengthening Latvia's position in the competition for investments.

Simplification and scope of examination

Among OECD countries, many differences exist between the amount and type of information needed, the type of control or legal check; name examination, use of public notary; and the submission format (paper, electronically).

In Latvia the scrutiny of the Registry is not substantive and rather procedural – e.g. verifying the correctness of the name and legal address of the applicant, and of the chosen name of the company - in the sense that the state notaries do not check the factual circumstances in which a certain decision was made, nor whether all facts specified in the submitted documents are true.[11] No scrutiny is performed at that stage on the type of economic activities envisaged by the applicant. The Registry may alert other public administrations such as the State Revenue Services about potential risky situations, in particular in relation to cases where an address appears to host several companies or where a person appears to sit on the board of several companies. The need to ensure that a legal entity can be reached at its legal address is the main reason why this check is conducted by the Enterprise Registry. Stakeholders mentioned it could also be used to avoid fraudulent behaviour in setting up companies at fake addresses (a non-existent building or a place where many other businesses are registered).

According to 50 business respondents, optimising the process and data requirement simplification is the main avenue for service improvement (Figure 3.6). As of October 2017, efforts were underway to simplify the registration process by reducing the number of issues checked by the Enterprise Registry as a pre-condition of registration. The issues the Registry should check were planned to be reduced to essentials, such as name, board composition, and whether the capital corresponds with the legal requirements. This is in line with stakeholders' recommendation for the Enterprise Registry to interfere less with regard to the substance of submitted applications. In particular, stakeholders preferred the Registry to engage less in checking the articles of association when registering a company.[12] It is recommended to monitor whether the reduction in intensity and breadth of the issues checked by the Registry is implemented in a way such that the mandate of the Registry and concerns of the users are satisfied.

In addition, where there are multiple enterprises registered at one address, the register entry is postponed for a certain number of days and stakeholders feel this loss of time unnecessary. Further, stakeholders felt that processes under which the Registry asks the State Revenue Service for further information could be streamlined. Such extra information may be required, for example, where there is only one board member.

Further simplifications might be considered, namely to simplify the law regarding the registration of branches of foreign companies in Latvia.

An "operate-straight" registration

From the point of view of future entrepreneurs, being able to swiftly operate should be the premise of the provision of registration services, i.e. taking into account pre-registration activities, to the registration per se and obtaining the necessary licences.

Building on the one-stop-shop approach, shifting from a concept of "simple administrative registration" to an "operate-ready" registration would ensure businesses are set up to perform their activities as soon as possible. This is in line with businesses that indicated in the survey the ability to obtain necessary business-related services in one location as a desired avenue for improvement. As mentioned above, registering your business entails some administrative activities that are out of the scope of the registration process at the Registry itself.

While checks are necessary to ensure the legality of the business activity, optimising data exchange between business services and integrating licencing services could improve business development in Latvia. For instance in the last ten years, the number of state and local government permits or licences and time spent to obtain them have increased.[13] Latvia is proposing to set up a single national body responsible for reviewing the licenses and permits related to business activities. Business development would gain in efficiency and effectiveness to see the operations of the proposed national body linked to the overall registration process.

Clear and up-to-date data for legal certainty

The first of these future developments is increasing the degree of publicity.

The Enterprise Registry currently provides publicity services that are in line with established international practice: 1) basic information is available free of cost (for example type of entity, legal address, name, registration number and date; 2) the remaining information is available at a fee not exceeding the administrative costs (this includes the documents on which registry entries are based); 3) private information providers use the information from the Enterprise Registry, enrich it with additional elements and offer these value-added services to interested parties (for example, information on liquidity and profitability).[14] Currently, such amendments are publicised in the National Gazette. Information about all amendments can be received by requesting a statement – full information about a registered legal entity (at a fee not exceeding the administrative costs). From the perspective of both cost reduction and accessibility improvement, it is suggested to move such publications to an electronic platform (only). For instance, the German Commercial Law provides for the online publication of register entries in its Section 10.[15]

An issue where certain progress was achieved, but which continues to plague the Enterprise Registry is a relatively large number of inactive companies on the Register. For example, by 31 May 2017, 262 108 entities were already registered, and out of those entities 179 315 were active, while over the course of 2010 only 262 004 entities were registered, out of which 179 271 were active. In turn, during the year 2009 the number of registered entities amounted to 261 922, out of which 179 240 were active (Baltic Legal, n.d.). While there is nothing to be said against using shelf companies that are created in order to be immediately ready if needed, stakeholder comments suggest that the inactive companies on the Enterprise Registry go far beyond the legitimate use of registering companies that are not immediately trading. In particular, such companies create a risk to be abused to the detriment of outsiders such as creditors. If this problem persists, it is suggested to consider using a combination of mixed measures to distinguish legitimate inactive companies from illegitimate ones. English law uses a mix of filing duties, penalties and the threat to strike companies from the register to deal with inactive companies (Box 3.4).

Box 3.4. Clearing the registry: UK practice

UK law requires inactive companies (so-called "dormant" companies) to file a confirmation statement and annual accounts with the register. If the company is dormant and small, the company may file "dormant accounts" instead and no auditors' report is required. A company is dormant if it had no significant transactions in the financial year. The sanctions for late or no filings are penalty payments and striking the company from the register.

For further information, see: www.gov.uk/government/publications/life-of-a-company-annual-requirements/life-of-a-company-part-1-accounts#dormant-company-accounts.

Legal empowerment and the use of ICT

The most significant barrier according to the 50 surveyed businesses was the complexity and vagueness of the information (Figure 3.5). While the procedures linked to registering a business are not perceived to be overly burdensome, information displayed on the Registry's website was by contrast not considered straightforward, which prompts several applicants to visit the Registry personally to ensure clarity.

The surveyed businesses requested more and clearer information on line, and, in addition, the ability to obtain information by phone (Figure 3.6). The Registry communication of the actual requirements and forms mandated in practice as opposed to the legal provisions set out in the Commercial Law is moreover reported to be a cause of confusion that prompts applicants to seek direct clarifications in person. The poor availability of information in English on relevant websites and brochures also impacts foreign applicants.

As users are more interested in a straightforward and cost-adequate registration process overall, other factors that affect registration, but are not necessarily in the competence of the Enterprise Registry, matter to them. Hence, the ease or difficulty of opening a bank account matters to users if this is a requirement for registration. A number of stakeholders mentioned that opening a bank account is difficult and hampers the registration process. The process of opening an account is perceived to require many documents and banks are thought to be quite restrictive in practice. When incorporating a company in Latvia, the founders have to physically go to the bank, which is a burden, and this is problematic in particular for foreign investors. Stakeholders wondered whether a framework could be put in place, under which a bank account is provided with ease once the essential elements for registration are provided.

As for other public services, information technology plays an important role for the future of the Enterprise Registry. Currently, electronic registration requires the use of an e-signature. Only 25% of businesses reported using e-signature in their dealings with the Enterprise Registry.[16] Users suggested pressing for the mandatory use of e-signatures to ensure the take up of this technology, similar to the Estonian experience. Current recognition by the Registry of e-signatures other than Latvian ones is very limited, even for some EU member states wherein interoperability is not established (with the exception of Estonia and Lithuania). Therefore, international investors encounter problems in the registration process. This is further complicated in cases where the foreign jurisdiction, e.g. China and Saudi Arabia, does not notarise foreign documents.

Stakeholders emphasised that their businesses do not only concern the European Union, but for them, investors are also attractive from the wider world. For example, when there is a change of shareholders, one physical document needs to travel through the world because the signatures need to be on one page. Stakeholders feel that the notary approach does not work well internationally. In addition, while a founder can certify his or her ID with an e-signature in Latvia, translators still physically need to go to the notary (also see the discussion above).

Use of the Registry's e-platform service grew from 38% in 2014 to 42% in 2016.[17] Users, however, reported problems when using the website registration service. A stakeholder involved in multiple registrations reported that as a consequence of the problems experienced, attaches all documents to an email and sends it to the Registry instead of using the e-platform. [18]Such cases are neither ideal for the user nor for the Registry. The e-platform offers efficiency advantages in terms of data transfer compared to other means of communication and, hence, it is in the interest of all parties involved for this e-platform approach to be used as extensively as possible. The introduction of e-addresses for enterprises is planned for 2020. Stakeholders suggested not to limit e-addresses to communication between enterprises and state agencies, but also to facilitate their use for communication between enterprises.

State Land Service and Land Registry offices

A reliable, transparent, complete and secure land registration system is associated with greater access to credit, lower income inequality and lower incidence of bribery at the Land Registry (World Bank, 2015). In Latvia, real estate and subsequent changes are recorded in Land Registries and the related property rights are registered in Land Books.

Organisational and service arrangements

Land administration system in Latvia is covered by two institutions – the State Land Service and the Land Registry. The State Land Service is supervised by the Ministry of Justice. The Land Registry offices are part of the district (city) court system: rights in the Land Registry are corroborated on the basis of a decision of a judge. The decision of the Land Registry office judge may be appealed in the Appeal Court.

State Land Service manages the National Real Estate Cadastre Information System (*Nekustamā īpašuma valsts kadastra informācijas sistēma*), which is used for registering the individual components of property and consolidating these components for the purpose of recording the property in the Land Registry. The State Land Service is headquartered in Riga with five regional offices. The Land Registry (*Zemesgrāmata*) is used for recording immovable property rights following registration of property in the National Real Estate Cadastral Information System.

Land Registries offices are judicial institutions and are maintained by the Court Administration (i.e. administrative work of Land Registry's offices). The State Single Computerised Land Registry groups the database of all the Land Registry offices. It contains the legally recognised information about the immovable properties and the rights related, as well as information on general issues, including easements and real estate encumbrances, landowners, the legal basis for the title, notifications on insolvency or creditor claims (European e-Justice, 2016). Information can be requested by specifically indicating the number of a division or the cadastre number of a property or the name of a property, or the address of an object in the composition of the property. Only the owner of an immovable property (and people who have certain rights to an immovable property) can examine immovable property folders and search immovable property by personal identification data.[19]

The separation of cadastre and land register into two entities – the State Land Service and the Land Register – creates challenges in terms of efficiency, consistency and accessibility. The dual structure may cause extra administrative costs, may lead to data inconsistency between the two institutions and may give rise to organisational complications. From the perspective of the users, it may be more complex and time-consuming to deal with two instead of one public service when it comes to land transactions. Some states such as Hungary and Lithuania solved these challenges by taking a unified approach where the cadastre and land register are organised in one institution. Other countries prefer a technology-based approach linking the registry and cadastre while keeping a dual structure. This approach needs to keep in mind that the issues to be solved do not only concern the organisational efficiency and data consistency of the cadastre and the register. In addition, the user perspective needs to be considered with a view to creating a one-stop-shop solution for land issues.

The division of the State Land Service (as part of the Executive) and the Land Registry (as part of the Judiciary) into two entities appears to be rooted in historical factors. Moving forward, as Latvia looks to identify efficiencies in the use of its judicial and state resources and to improve accessibility of state and justice services to users, Latvia may consider greater use of legal clerks in dealing with land registration issues and possibly strengthening the connection between the two entities. Many OECD countries can provide good examples in this regard. Many countries have merged the services under the roof of one state agency, although some OECD countries have their Land Registry managed by the Judiciary. In Germany, the Land Registry may be accessed only by persons who can show a legitimate interest in consulting it (e.g. particularly for legal or economic reasons). To do so, they must first contact the Land Registry office in the district in which the property is located. Those persons may also apply for excerpts. These restricted groups of users that may consult the Land Registry data via an electronic portal for the particular federal state include German courts, public authorities, notaries, credit institutions and utility companies. The judicial authorities of the federal states are responsible for regulating these access rights (European e-Justice, 2015).

Accessing the service in practice

Registering a property in Latvia is a three-stage process. First, the business will verify the title of the real estate and the legal rights attached on line, by paying a fee of EUR 5.[20] After the parties sign a real estate sales agreement, they submit it to the municipality for a decision on its first refusal rights. After notarising its application, it is submitted to a land book judge for registration. The entry in the Land Registry should be made no longer than within ten days. According to the authorities, it usually takes five to six days. After examination of a request for corroboration, it is certified by a decision of the judge in a Land Registry office and immediately entered into the computerised Land Registry. Supporting documents can be sent by post to the Land Registry office.

Stakeholders are generally satisfied with the services provided by the State Land Service and the Land Registry offices. Specifically, most of the survey respondents expressed rather positive experiences with the institutions (19 out of 32). There is, however, disparity in the assessment of the staff in the State Land Registry offices – it was said to be knowledgeable and competent while some respondents strongly disagreed. Surveyed businesses (32) highlighted four main barriers: accessibility and vagueness of the information; the complexity of the process and language; financial and time burden (Figure 3.7). As for the financial costs, further analysis is needed to better capture the financial burden beyond the service fee.

Figure 3.7. Main barriers to accessing the services of the Land Registry Offices

Based on 74 replies out of 80 from 32 businesses

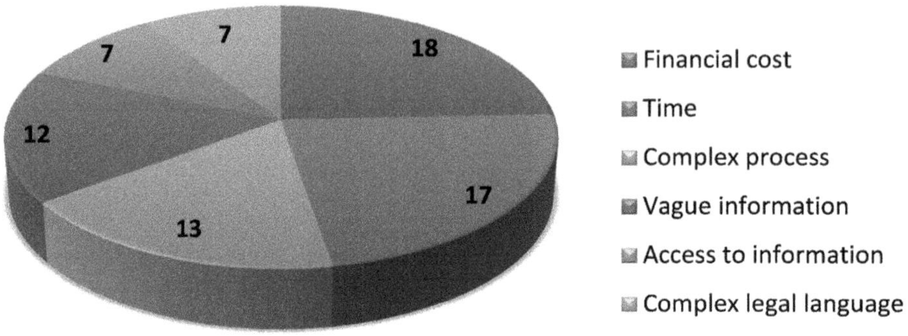

Source: OECD (2017a).

According to the survey of the Ministry of Economy, in 2016 it took on average 16.5 (and up to 42.1) days to register real estate in Latvia compared to 24 days in 2014. According to the Office, the latest data from the year 2017 show that in Land Registry offices in Riga the application, when submitted, is decided within 5.7 days on average. The 32 surveyed businesses questioned as part of this report indicated that the process took less than 1 day to 1 week (10) and from 1 week to 1 month (18).

Avenues for service improvement according to surveyed businesses

Pre-registration activities, i.e. preparing the paperwork, were seen as mostly burdensome by 32 businesses. Respondents reported lengthy procedures that could be improved by simplifying data requirements and process and number of steps (Figure 3.8).

Figure 3.8. Main avenues for service improvement of the Land Registry

Based on 103 replies from 32 businesses

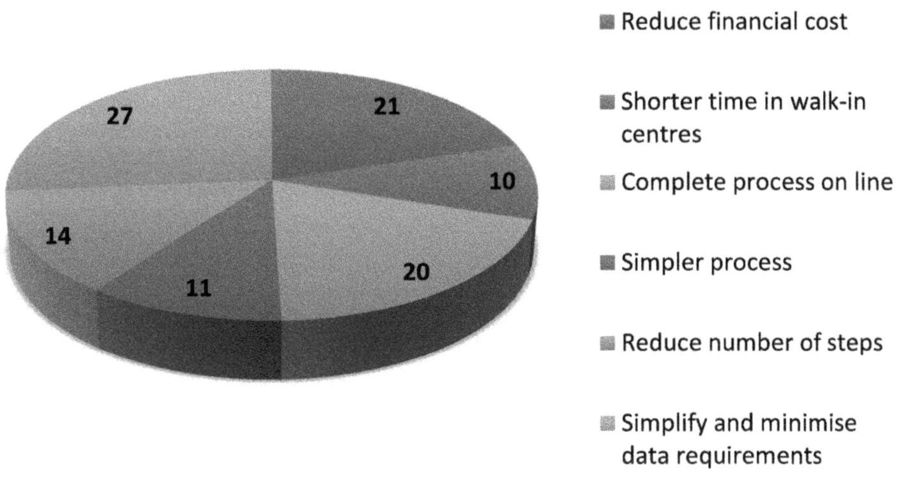

Source: OECD (2017a).

Unifying the Land Registry services

It is suggested to reconsider the division of land services into two entities against the advantages of centralising both services in one institution. This can promise costs savings and facilitate the provision of one-stop-shop services to users (see below). Indeed in some economies, having the real property registration and information gathered in one system shows positive outcomes by limiting inconsistency and ensuring more comprehensive data provision. According to the World Bank (2015), doing so helps maintain up-to-date records on the legal rights to properties and the spatial characteristics of land plots, thus increasing tenure security. It also provides a single point of contact for those conducting land transactions.

Enhancing the use of land and cadastral e-services

Despite significant improvements in the automation of information and registration by Latvian authorities, it is important that the current system continues its efforts towards comprehensive and efficient access to land and cadastral services, using information and communication technologies (ICTs). Many entrepreneurs do not seem to use electronic means to apply for registrations with the Land Registry (10% in 2016, mostly in Riga).[21] As confirmed in the survey, most businesses stated that they went in person to the Land Registry office to handle their cases (26 out of 32 respondents). The need for the development of e-services in order to facilitate the completion of a process on line was highlighted (Figure 3.7). Banks, instead, were said to use electronic registration regularly. It is suggested to create the necessary framework and incentivise stakeholders other than banks to use electronic registration, including reviewing the need for notarised documents. Furthermore, it may prove fruitful to explore the digital registration of mortgages and similar instruments to provide an efficient background for credit security.[22]

Patent Office

Latvia is focusing on improving its patent system in a bid to boost innovation activity and research and development (R&D) expenditure.[23] Providing firms with well-defined and high-quality intellectual property (IP) rights and enforcement mechanisms for those rights is necessary (OECD, 2017a). Intellectual property rights give businesses an incentive to invest in R&D, encouraging the creation of innovative products and processes. They also give their holders the confidence to share new technologies through – among other things – joint ventures and licensing agreements. In this way, successful innovations are, in time, diffused within and across economies, bringing higher productivity and growth (OECD, 2010b).

Organisational and service arrangements

The Patent Office of the Republic of Latvia (*Latvijas Republikas Patentu valde*) is the central authority in the Latvian industrial property protection system. It administers the grants of national patents and the filing and validation of some European patent applications. Latvia is also a member of the Enhanced Co-operation on the Unitary Patent Protection and ratified the Unified Patent Court (UPC). The Patent Office provides for the registration of trademarks, design, topographies of semiconductor products and supplementary protection certificates. Businesses and other stakeholders can also register their trademarks under the Madrid system since 1993 and their designs and models under the Hague system since 2005. The service is centralised in Riga and e-services are available.

The Patent Office offers free access to up-to-date information on registered IP rights, the current legal status of Latvian trademarks, and industrial design registrations. It is part of the European Trade Mark and Design Network, which provides trademark and design statistics; a common user satisfaction system; an enforcement database; and e-learning for small and medium-sized enterprises (Box 3.5). None of the 53 business respondents found the process complex or difficult to understand or were lost in the process.

Box 3.5. The European Trade Mark and Design Network

The European Trade Mark and Design Network (ETMDN) is the hub that connects national and regional intellectual property offices, user associations and other relevant organisations from all across Europe. The network provides a high-quality experience for users of the IP system by having up-to-date electronic services, facilitates access to information, and converges practices on how IP offices examine and evaluate trademarks and designs. The projects are driven by working groups made of experts from the participating institutions. Infrastructure and resources to support project implementation are provided by the European Union Intellectual Property Office and the participating IP offices.

There are several intellectual property tools aimed at supporting examiners, businesses and the enforcement community available on the ETMDN website. For instance, the "TM view" allows any person to search for, free of charge, the trademarks of all the trademark offices involved in the initiative. The "Design view" is a centralised access point to view the registered design information held by any of the participating national offices. The ETMDN website also makes available e-learning courses providing online training for small and medium-sized enterprises on the importance of IP rights.

Source: European Trade Mark and Design Network website.

Accessing the service in practice

Registration process

In Latvia the granting of national patents is an easy procedure as it is a simple registration procedure. Among businesses that have declared having used the Patent Office to obtain legal protection of an invention (7 out of 53) or trademarks (7 out of 49) in the last three years, most respondents were satisfied if not very satisfied with the service provided. When a patent application with respective documentation is submitted, the Patent Office examines the documents and determines whether the filed documents conform to the requirements of patent law. If the submitted documents conform, the Patent Office sets the patent application filing date. The Patent Office proceeds to a formal examination of the application within three months, after which the date is set for publication of the application. The publication shall be made within 18 months of the filing date or – if priority was requested – from the earlier priority date of the application. This enables the applicant to file an application in other countries within 12 months as well as to obtain the results of the search informing the applicant about the patentability of the invention before publication. After the fee is paid by the applicant, the Patent Office registers the patent in the State Patent Register, publishes the notification regarding the grant of a patent in the Official Gazette of the Patent Office (available only on the official website of the Patent Office) and issues the patent to the owner of the patent. The 53 survey respondents stated that this procedure is time-consuming and significantly impedes the use of services provided by the institution (4 out of 6). Nevertheless, no businesses reported difficulties in understanding or following the process; the paperwork was also not seen as burdensome. The staff of the Patent Office were said to be knowledgeable and competent by all respondents (3). The decisions of the Patent Office are appealable (Gencs Valters Law Firm, 2016) (see Box 3.13 later in this chapter for more information).

The patentability of the invention is tested in the course of court proceedings when challenged (Box 3.13). This approach helps not to deter potential businesses from applying for a patent. Applications can be filed in English, French, German, Russian or any other EU official language under a European patent application, provided a Latvian translation of the invention formula (claims) is submitted within three months. Patent searches are free.

The ability to complete the process on line was seen as limited for two out of four business respondents, and considered an avenue to be further explored.

E-service

The experience of the Patent Office with e-applications of trademarks and designs demonstrates the advantages of e-platform services over e-signature services. Relevant cost savings are made with the e-platform approach while with e-signatures, little savings are achieved. It is suggested to consider whether the discount of 10% for electronic applications could be increased where higher savings are made, for example in the case of e-platform applications, under certain circumstances. The last cost assessment was performed in 2015. A starting point would be to recalculate costs per service, as envisioned by Ministry of Finance, "A pilot project to reduce the costs of processing patent applications and to improve their quality was launched by the Patent Office in October 2016" (OECD, 2017b).

Service costs for users

According to information provided by the Patent Office, fees to file a patent application or an application for an additional protection certificate is EUR 120 (patent application costs vary based on the number of claims and the number of pages in the application; discounts are available for physical disability [60%] or a student or retiree [80%]); EUR 90 for granting a patent and patent publication; EUR 90 to EUR 420 for a renewal. Fees to file a trademark application start from EUR 90 for an individual trademark and EUR 150 for a collective trademark; EUR 95 for registration; EUR 180 for renewal of an individual trademark and EUR 240 for a collective trademark. Regarding designs, the minimum fee to file a national application for a single design is EUR 40; EUR 65 for registration and publication (only one representation in an application) including the grant of the registration certificate and between EUR 170 and EUR 335 renewal fees depending on the renewal period.

Other service costs related to the work of international IP institutions are the following: preparation of a community design application and forwarding it to the European Union Intellectual Property Office (EUR 31); preparation of a priority document on the basis of documents and materials from the Patent Office's register and transmitting it to the International Bureau of the World Intellectual Property Office (EUR 19.16).

The Patent Office's service costs for the legal protection of trademarks were seen either as affordable (4 out of 6 respondents) or expensive (2). Thus, it was suggested to reduce the financial burden of registration.

A continuum of dispute resolution services

Service chain and user-centricity

OECD work on access to justice focuses on users trying to identify and address their legal needs through a full continuum of legal and justice services (Figure 3.9). Evidence indicates that exclusive reliance on litigation through the judiciary system can be costly (both to the state and litigants) and lengthy. With this view, countries are taking steps to promote a wide range of legal and justice services, recognising that effective resolution of disputes can take place through various pathways to justice, which could be arrayed along a continuum of services from access to alternative dispute resolution (ADR) mechanisms to full litigation, and from access to legal information and legal advice to full representation.

Figure 3.9. A continuum of legal and justice services

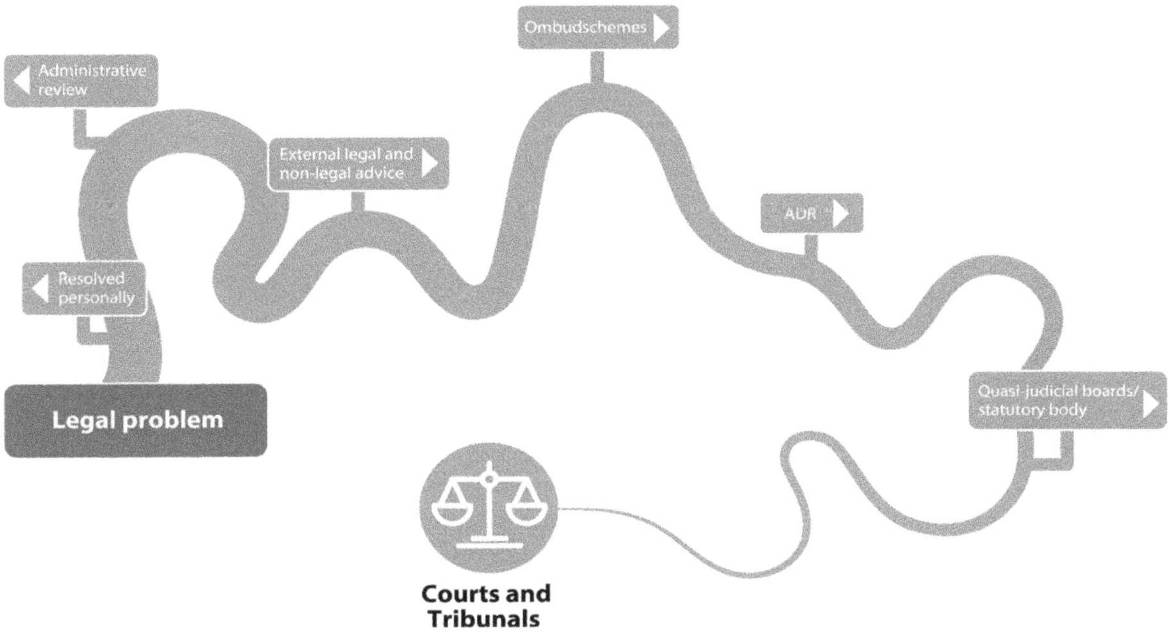

Source: Adapted from Australia - Attorney-General's Department (2009).

Justice and legal assistance are recognised as a public service in most OECD countries. The user-centred perspective should be incorporated in a broad range of modalities to resolve legal problems. The concept of the expanded rule of law envisions accessible procedures that enable fair outcomes for all, and particularly those who live in situations of disadvantage or vulnerability, whose cases rarely reach a courtroom.

The experience of OECD member countries underscores the importance of several criteria to ensure efficient justice service delivery adapted to people's legal needs from entry to the endpoint of the justice continuum. These include: evidence-based planning, inclusion, empowerment, prevention and timeliness, responsiveness, collaboration and integration, outcome focus, fairness and effectiveness. These criteria can be implemented across all the components of the justice system: structures, processes, outcomes, and the system as a whole, and assist by: improving data-collecting capacity; building stakeholder support and ownership; informing project design; gauging project effectiveness and informing practice; increasing transparency and accountability; and including the perspectives of vulnerable groups (Figure 3.10).

Figure 3.10. Common criteria for service delivery

Source: OECD (2017b).

Businesses' legal needs and behaviour in Latvia

As part of this report, Latvia conducted a business legal needs survey.[24] While assessing the legal needs and experience of citizens is gathering some strong interest among OECD and non-OECD countries, a smaller number of countries carried out this innovative approach to help better tailor the delivery of justice services to the specific needs of the study subjects (Box 3.6). In practice, this exercise seeks not only to identify the legal problems of businesses but to also understand how they face this problem, what action if any they took and why, and what the underlying causes and consequences were. The analysis in the following sections builds on four complementary tools: an online legal need and experience survey conducted for the purpose of this report; interviews with governmental and non-governmental stakeholders; official information provided by Latvia; and a literature review. A total of 295 business representatives participated in the overall survey on access to business justice services with 62 responding to the legal needs and experience section. These data represent the views of a small number of businesses and should be interpreted with caution.

Box 3.6. Business legal needs studies in OECD countries

In the **United Kingdom** (England and Wales), the Small Business Legal Needs Benchmarking Survey conducted in 2013 highlighted the direct relevance of addressing the legal issues of businesses to improve the business environment and promote economic growth. The survey collected information on the characteristics of small businesses; internal legal expertise and the practice of using legal services; legal problems faced by small businesses including nature, model, impact and outcome; the strategies to address legal issues; attitudes to law, regulation and services.

In the **Netherlands**, the Ministry of Safety and Justice conducted two surveys that aimed to identify difficulties experienced by small and medium-sized companies. The study focused on the occurrence and settlement of (potential) legal problems in those companies, which jointly makes up over 99% of the companies in the country. The research focussed on the nature and frequency of the problems; legal pathways chosen; legal assistance providers and final solutions to the problems.

The **Australian** Department for Industry, Innovation and Science was created to enable growth and productivity for globally competitive industries. Its work focuses on supporting science and commercialisation, growing business investment and improving business capability, streamlining regulation and building a high-performance organisation. The Office of the Chief Economist provides publicly accessible data on resources, energy, innovation and industry. It serves as a basis for numerous publications and research papers addressing a wide range of economic issues. For instance, most recently, analysis of entrepreneurship dynamics in Australia was published.

Source: Pleasence, P. and N.J. Balmer (2013); Netherlands - Ministry of Safety and Justice website; Australia - Department for Industry, Innovation and Science website.

Characteristics and impact of legal issues faced by Latvian businesses

Legal interactions with other businesses, customers or the government are the backbone of business activities ranging from employment, intellectual property protection, leasing premises, etc. Latvian businesses mostly deal with other businesses (165 respondents) or customers (134 respondents) in their everyday activities. Their business dealings with the government amount to almost 20% of their interactions. Those legal relationships are potential sources of legal threat for businesses in all OECD countries. While all types of businesses are affected, small businesses are particularly prone to volatility, and misfortune that could lead to legal issues (Pleasence and Balmer, 2017a). Additionally, a US study found that the larger the business, the higher the proportion of disputes (Norton Rose Fulbright, 2017). In some countries, businesses feel increasingly exposed to cybersecurity and data-protection-related disputes (Norton Rose Fulbright, 2017).

In Latvia, 39 out of 62 business respondents reported having encountered at least one legal problem in the past two years. The most frequently experienced problems relate to employment (e.g. payment of wages/pension, staff misconduct and dismissal or threat of dismissal), followed by regulations (e.g. data protection, filing/content of annual company accounts, need for/outcome of audit, mandatory licenses/permits/accreditation or insurance) and goods or services provided to customers or purchased by the business (late, partial or non-payment).

Figure 3.11. Types of problems faced by businesses in Latvia in the last 24 months

Based on 353 replies from 62 businesses

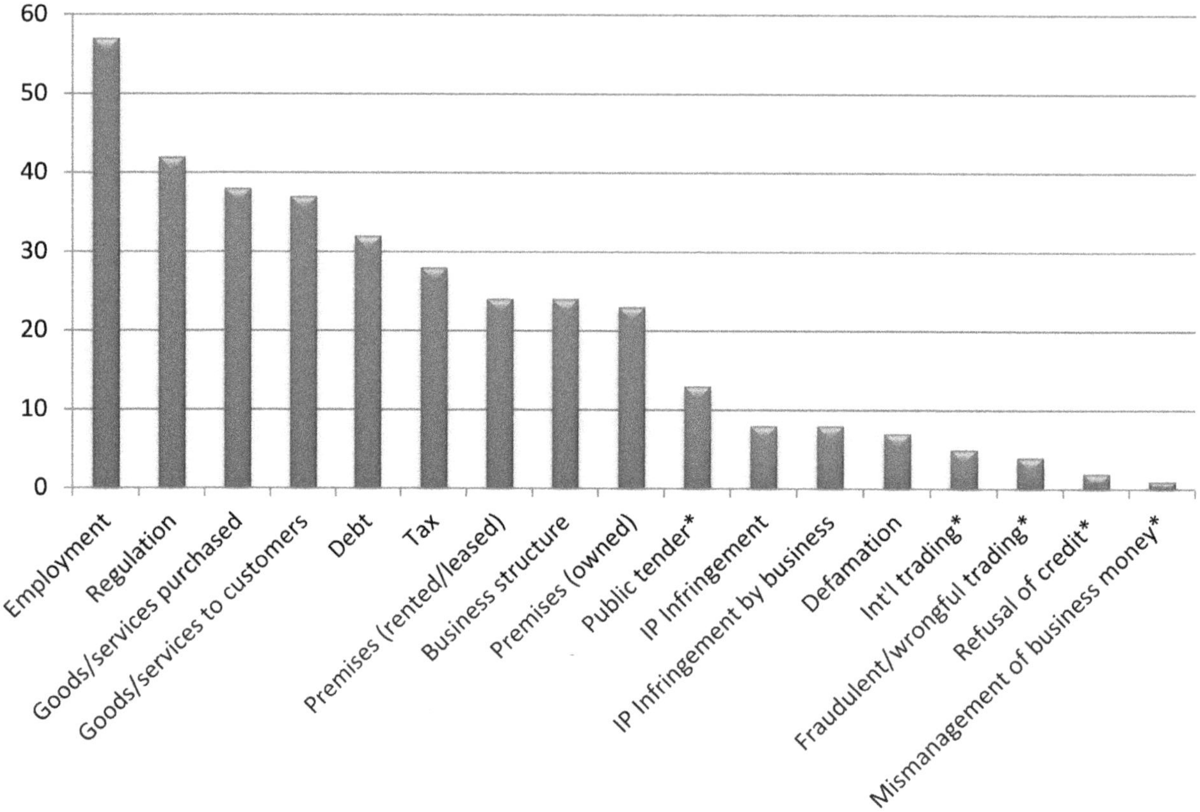

Notes:
Fraudulent or wrongful trading: Concerning insolvency
Public tender: Unfair operation
Int'l trading: Legal/regulatory issue
Refusal of credit: Due to incorrect information held by a credit reporting agency
Mismanagement of business money including of investments by financial services
Source: OECD (2017a).

The prevalence of a legal issue is not correlated to the level of concern of business. The nature of the problem and the perception of its seriousness can vary, thus being a deciding factor in the course of action (see below).

Based on 44 replies, business respondents were said to be most affected by legal problems linked to the unfair operation of a public tender (11.36%), liability for tax/amount of tax owed (11.36%), payment for good or services (9.09%), or fraudulent or wrongful trading (concerning insolvency) (6.82%). In the five largest business sectors, the unfair operation of tender and liability to tax were said to carry the highest consequences (Figure 3.12). It would be interesting to further the analysis and understand the factor of concerns (e.g. time, legal cost, reputational risk, etc.).

Figure 3.12. Most significant legal problems in the five largest surveyed business sectors in Latvia

Based on 129 replies from 29 businesses

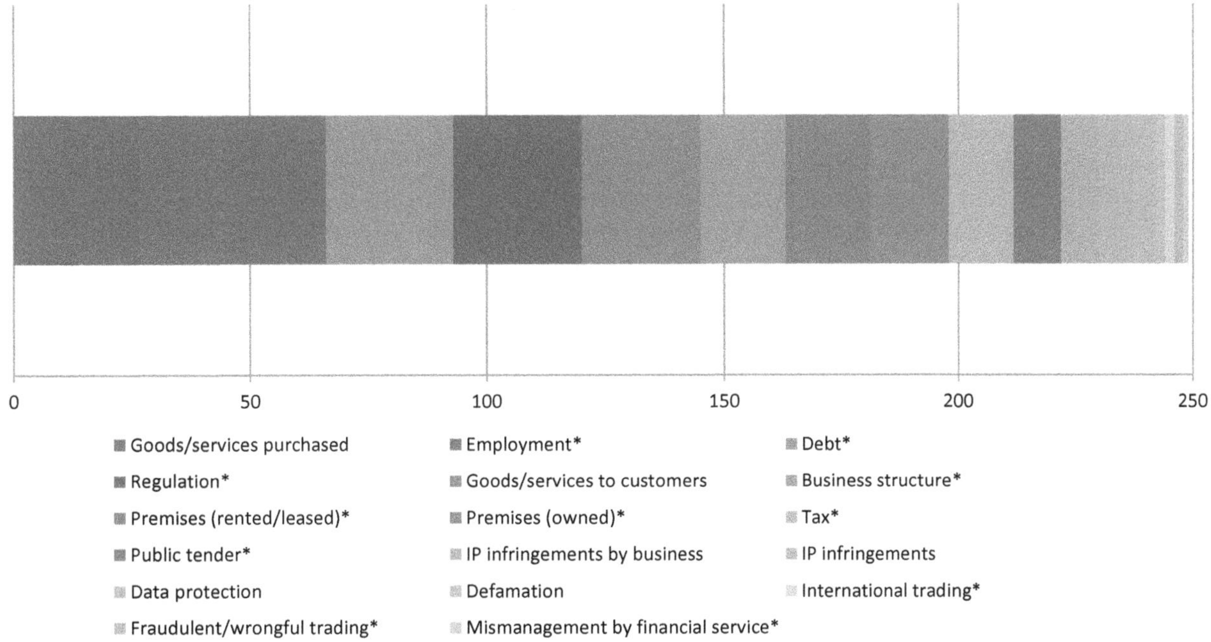

Notes:
Five largest surveyed business sectors: Manufacturing; Information and communication; Wholesale and retail trade, repair of motor vehicles and motorcycles; Financial and insurance activities; Real estate, renting and business activities.
Employment: e.g. Payment of wages/pension; Staff misconduct; Staff dismissal (or threat); Exercise of parental rights (including maternity), leave/pay or flexible working request
Debt: e.g. Administration; Receivership; Debt relief order
Regulation: e.g. Filing/content of annual company accounts; Need for/outcome of the audit; Mandatory insurance
Business structure: e.g. Change of legal status; Technicalities of business start-up; Sale of business
Premises (rented/leased): e.g. Rent arrears; Terms of rental agreement/lease
Premises (owned): e.g. Repairs/maintenance of communal areas; Conveyancing
Tax: e.g. Tax liability; Errors in business tax return; Failure to register/report changes
Public tender: Unfair operation
International trading: Legal/regulatory issue
Fraudulent/wrongful trading: Concerning insolvency
Mismanagement of business money /investments by financial service
Source: OECD (2017a).

Inability to resolve legal problems may have a negative knock-on effect for the business and its owner(s). Some studies concluded that businesses suffer financial cost (e.g. loss of income; incurring of additional costs), social costs (e.g. upset within the business; damage to employee relations) or reputational costs (e.g. damage to business relationships, loss of reputation), and in extreme cases, businesses ceasing trading (Blackburn, Kitching and Saridakis, 2015).

Legal issues in the professional domain may compound other legal problems and have a spillover effect on the personal life and health of business owners (e.g. stress), especially of SMEs (Pleasence and Balmer, 2017b; Blackburn, Kitching and Saridakis, 2015). In turn, illness and relationship breakdowns are identified as potential triggers for business difficulties leading to liquidation in the worst case scenario.[25] While further analysis is necessary to measure the impact of business-related problems intertwined with non-business ones, by way of an illustration "in England and Wales, the economic value of this impact was suggested to amount to tens of billions of pounds per year" (Blackburn, Kitching and Saridakis, 2015; Pleasence and Balmer, 2017b).

In Latvia unresolved legal problems mostly impacted businesses' revenue directly or indirectly; businesses also reported missed opportunities. The economic cost may be significant to the business market valuation and value, competitiveness and growth: the average estimated monetary value of legal problems declared by 25 respondents amounted to EUR 2.5 million, ranging from EUR 35 to 50 million. Additionally, a study revealed that the announcement of a filing might bear wealth losses for businesses (listed companies) due to "increased probability of financial distress.[26]

Figure 3.13. Adversarial impact of the most significant legal problems for businesses in Latvia in the last 24 months

Based on 96 replies from 37 businesses

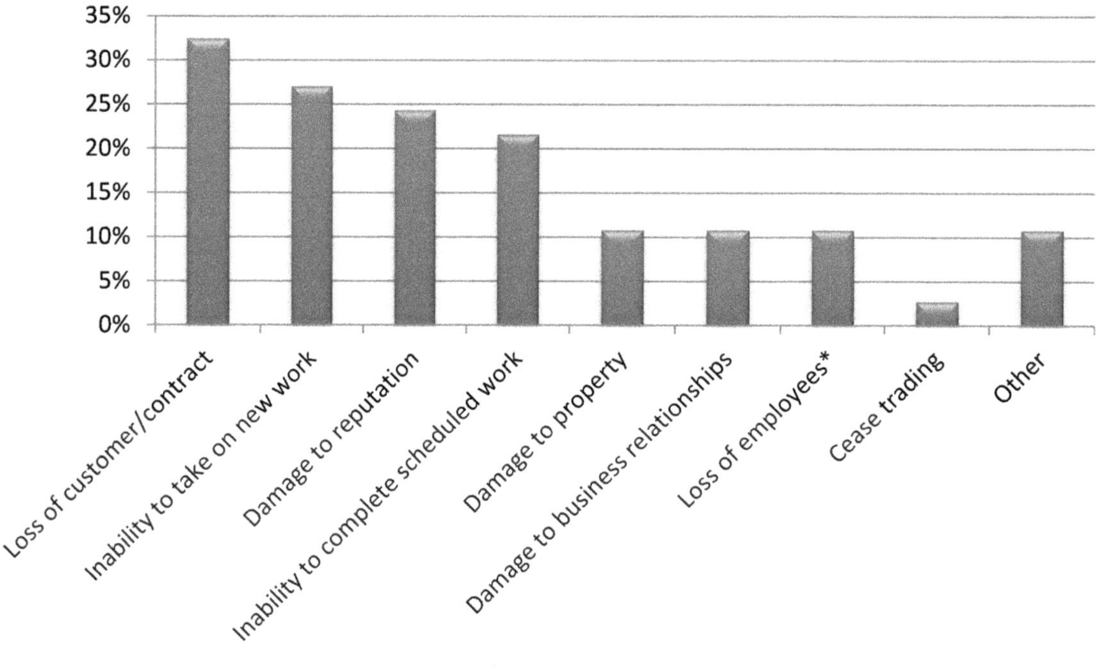

Note:
Additional costs: e.g. Increased insurance costs
Loss of employees: Other than through dismissal/redundancy
Source: OECD (2017a).

Response strategies to businesses' legal problems

As mentioned above, the nature and the perceived or real seriousness of the problem can influence how a business addresses its legal difficulties. For instance a study commissioned by the Australian Department of Innovation, Industry, Science and Research (DIISR) highlighted that businesses in such situations distinguished between issues that are "routine and minor, not something to worry about"; "potentially serious but easily resolved without escalation"; "potentially serious but avoided escalation due to potential costs"; "serious enough to consider utilising third-party intervention but did not actually do so"; "of a nature that required intervention by a third party or self-representation in formal proceedings" to "serious enough to result in legal action being taken by either business involved in the dispute" (Orima Research, 2010).

In OECD countries, businesses seek to prevent potential legal disputes or minimise the problem as part of the process (Figure 3.14).

Figure 3.14. Dispute prevention and resolution process framework

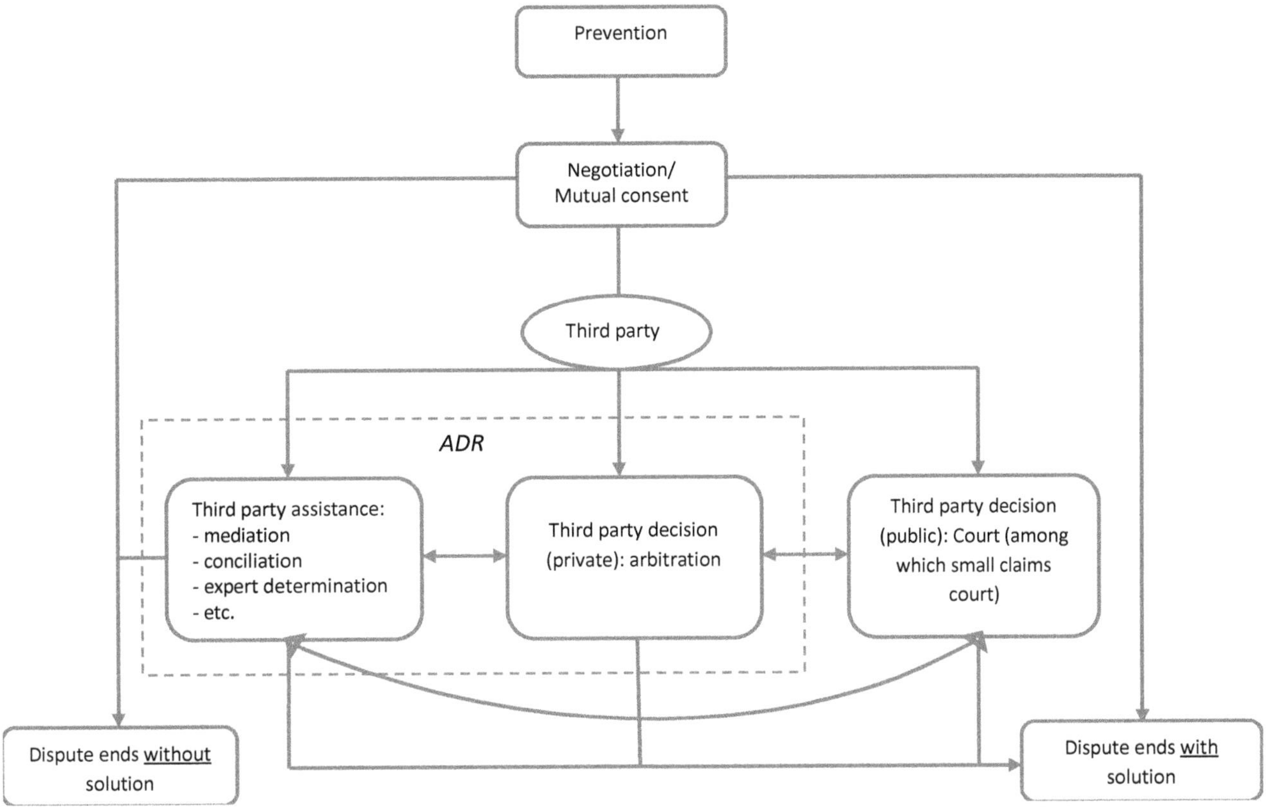

Source: Adapted from van der Horst, R., R. de Vree and P. van der Zeijden (2006).

Risk reduction measures used involve regular training; quality schemes; background checks of a potential business partner; and contract reviews (van der Horst, de Vree and van der Zeijden, 2006; Norton Rose Fulbright, 2017) (Figure 3.15). Business in a 2016 study lauded internal training as the most effective preventive measure (Norton Rose Fulbright, 2017). Businesses will also often reach out to the other party to settle the matter whether before instigating formal or informal dispute resolution proceedings or during the litigation process. For instance, micro-enterprises and SMEs brought on average less than 40% of intellectual property disputes cases before the UK Patents Court between 2003 and 2009 (IPO, 2010).[27] The study reported that 40% of listed cases are settled while 50% are heard by a judge. It highlighted that negotiation was preferred over mediation and litigation.[28] A potential explanation could be found in the social environment and networks that may influence the way an SME handles its legal issues, i.e. which mechanisms to elect - formal or informal or procedural approach (e.g. adjudicatory or conciliatory) (Gómez, 2008). Family-owned businesses may rely more often on non-formal ADR mechanisms and talk the matter out directly with the other party in view of protecting the business relationship in the long term (Gómez, 2008). These businesses would turn to formal legal advice sources once having exhausted their network and trusted sources (Blackburn, Kitching and Saridakis, 2015). Some businesses in OECD countries will also preventively purchase insurance policies to cover for potential legal expenses. Yet the cost and lack of awareness of these policies seemed to inhibit their adoption.[29]

Figure 3.15. Framework for minimising disputes

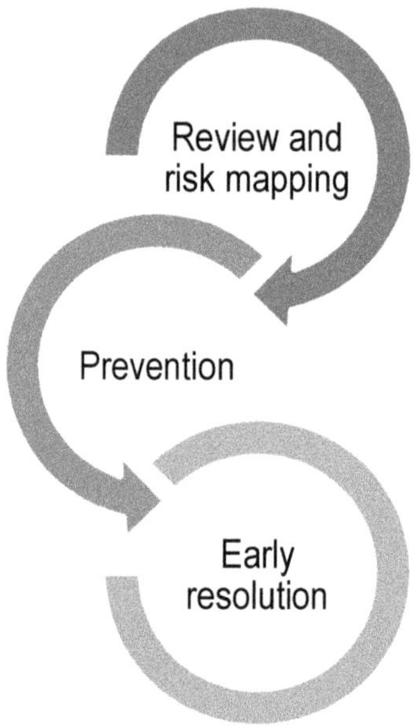

Source: Adapted from Norton Rose Fulbright (2017).

In Latvia, business seems to more often than not confront their legal problems. The 42 business respondents including family-owned businesses chose to sort the problem out on their own (47.62% and 48%) rather than retaining external professional help (28.5% and 24%). Only 7.14% of businesses took advantage of governmental information sources (Figure 3.16).

Figure 3.16. How Latvian businesses address their legal problems

Based on 42 business respondents

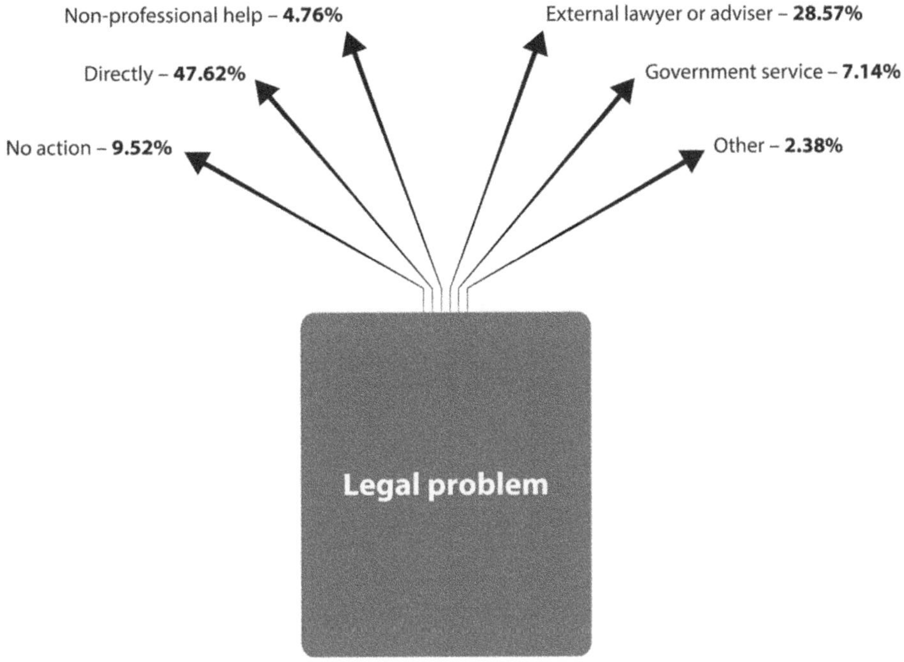

Source: OECD (2017a).

In Latvia, as in many OECD countries, businesses contemplate a wide array of avenues to address their legal plight. Yet this variety of often disconnected dispute resolution services can be overwhelming, especially for non-legal specialists. Different services bear different direct or indirect costs: financial or opportunistic. As a study contends: "There is an inherent irony in the judicial system in that individuals who bring suit may endure injury from the very process through which they seek redress. The legal process itself is often a trauma" (Strasburger, 1999).

Some studies observed that while SMEs may encounter fewer legal difficulties than larger companies due to the small scale of their activities, they are said to be less capable of facing and resolving them.[30] This can have an impact on the favourability of the outcome.[31]

Over half of overall respondents stated possessing the internal legal capacity, mostly in company or contract law (138 out of 258 respondents). Yet over half of the family-owned businesses reported otherwise. Moreover, on deciding on the course of action, business respondents including family-owned businesses who decide not to seek redress cited time considerations (and not legal awareness).

Figure 3.17. How Latvian businesses resolve their legal problems

Based on 22 replies from 17 businesses

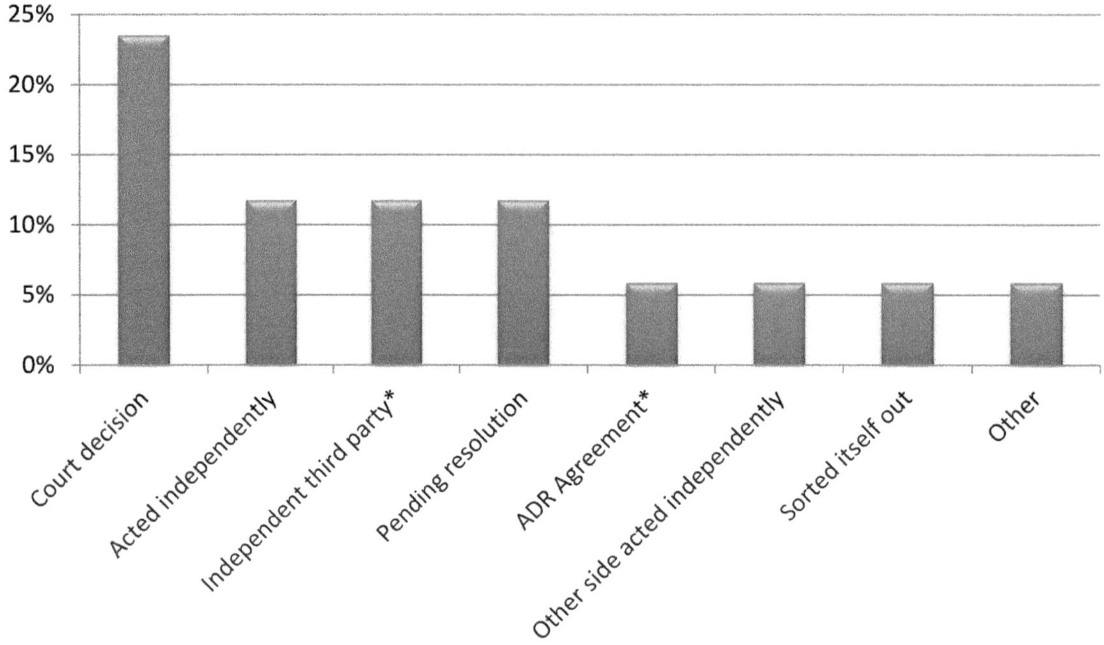

Notes:
Independent third party: Action or decision of an independent third party, e.g. police, regulator
ADR Agreement: Judicial or non-judicial
Business representation: Agreement reached through a representative of the business (e.g. solicitor or accountant)
Source: OECD (2017a).

Length of time (whether linked to the proceedings or to the dealing of the dispute) appears to be the main impediment for businesses who acted upon their problem (Figure 3.18). Financial costs were particularly highlighted by family-owned business respondents. Further developments on the experience with dispute recourse mechanisms in Latvia are described below.

Figure 3.18. Most significant barriers faced by Latvian businesses in resolving legal problems

Based on 96 replies from 34 businesses

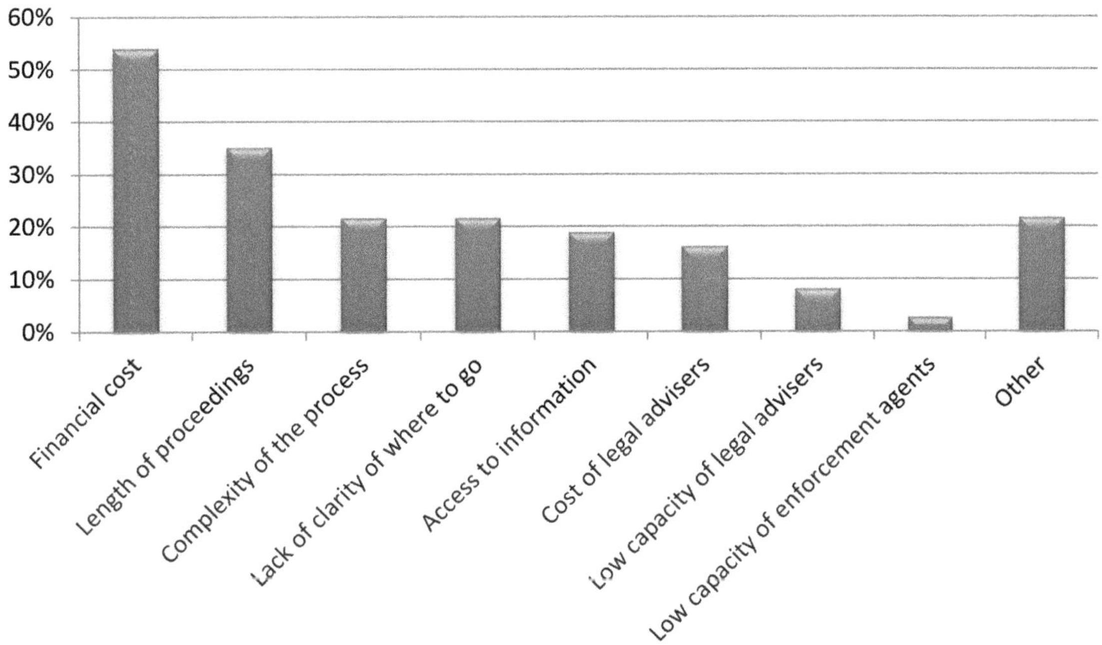

Source: OECD (2017a).

Access to user-centred dispute resolution mechanisms in Latvia

Surveyed businesses felt unsatisfied with the pathway chosen to address their legal problem (7 respondents). Yet they are equally satisfied or very unsatisfied. They highlighted different ways to improve their experience (Figure 3.19) including:

- improving/creating online services to access legal information;
- simplifying the data requirements.

Figure 3.19. Main avenues for the improvement of the dispute resolution system in Latvia

Based on 42 replies from 28 businesses

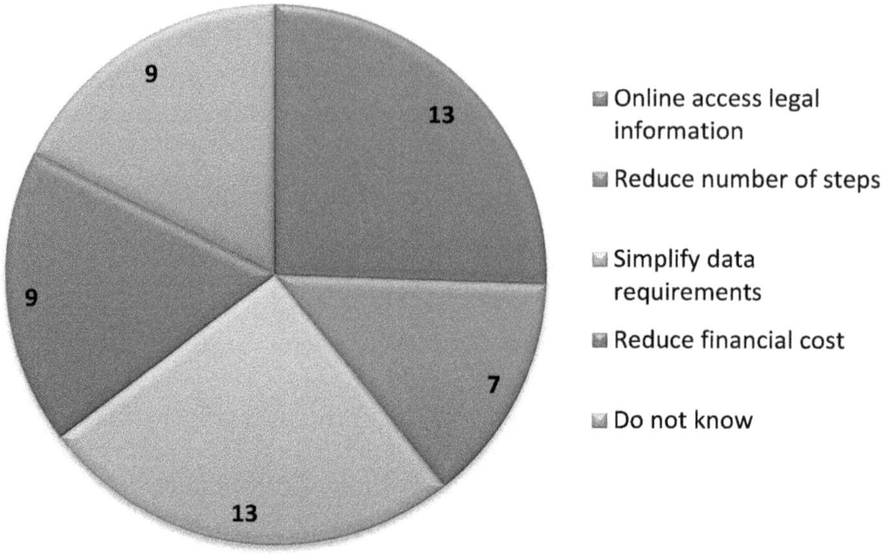

Source: OECD (2017a).

Access to the court system

The Latvian court system underwent a comprehensive reform to establish a "clear three-level instance system" by 2016 (CEPEJ, 2018).[32] Under the ordinary jurisdiction framework, civil and criminal are heard before district (city) courts (*rajonu [pilsētu] tiesa*) at the first instance jurisdiction and by regional courts (*apgabaltiesas*) at the appellate level. Administrative district (city) and regional courts review the legality and validity of acts and actions of administrative authorities or institutions.[33] The Supreme Court (*Augstākā tiesa*) serves as the cassation instance for all three sectors of justice.

Over one-third of businesses surveyed stated that their most significant legal problem terminated before a judge (37 respondents). This proportion rose to over 75% for family-owned enterprises. Businesses mainly completed the process in person or by post. Improving trust is seen as an essential factor by almost 50% of business respondents, which is a key requirement for the Supreme Court in the implementation of its judicial reforms.[34] Moreover, stakeholders highlighted three key challenges similar to the ones experienced in other OECD countries.

Box 3.7. Duration, cost and complexity of judicial proceedings in OECD countries

Duration, cost and complexity of litigation procedures are considered among the top barriers, particularly for SMEs. Therefore, several countries have developed e-services in order to reduce judicial proceedings' duration and enhance their transparency.

In **Korea**, the e-court experience shows significant outcomes towards fairer and faster trials for companies, with a particular impact on small enterprises' access to justice. The electronic-case filing system allows for electronic filing of civil, commercial, administrative and family affairs cases since 2010. These e-court solutions include features to help judges in judicial proceedings, facilitating the filing of cases for litigants, and informing the public about case outcomes.

In Texas (**United States**), a majority of courts have implemented the e-Filing for Courts system, which facilitates the two-way flow of judicial information between all relevant stakeholders (attorneys, clerks, court personnel and judges). The system "exports directly to an existing document management system (DMS)", thus allowing to "barcode, index, and store each electronic filing automatically" and therefore "reducing the amount of time clerk and court personnel spend on these activities".

British Columbia's (**Canada**) eCourt Initiative developed an integrated case management system and publicly accessible e-services. This programme was a joint initiative of the Ministry of the Attorney General of British Columbia, the British Columbia Court Services Branch and the three levels of the BC judiciary. It aimed to provide an integrated system facilitating "seamless co-ordination from e-documents created in law offices to the registry to the judicial desktop and the courtroom, which would include eCourtrooms" having a complete e-court file. The objectives of this initiative were to support "public access (including e-searches, online document purchase, court lists, e-filing and a filing assistant), out-of-court access by justice partners such as crown attorneys, police and defence counsel (including document production, routing, signing and distribution), and in-court functionalities".

The Money Claim Online (MCOL) is an online service for the e-filing of money claims in **England** and **Wales**. It enables English and Welsh citizens and lawyers to issue a money claim through a user-friendly website which "allows for filing documents, checking claim status, and requesting both judgement entry and enforcement (by way of a warrant of execution)".

As a supranational model, the **European Union**'s e-CODEX (e-Justice Communication via Online Data Exchange) project "improves the cross-border access of citizens and businesses to legal means in Europe and furthermore creates the interoperability between legal authorities within the European Union". In this framework, several civil justice pilots started being implemented in 2013, focusing on European Payment Order, small claims, and business registers.

Source: OECD (2015d); World Bank (2014); TexasOnline--eFiling for Courts, website; Lupo, G and J.Bailey (2014); e-CODEX website.

Complexity

Most of the 37 business surveyed knew where to go or whom to contact to handle an issue. Yet they still felt unsure of what to do. While most respondents declared the application process to be straightforward, 5 out of 11 businesses respondents further found the process to be complex. The complexity of the process and language represented a significant barrier for 8 out 11 respondents. The lack of accessibility and the vagueness of the information may have contributed to the situation (6 out of 11 respondents). Consideration should be given to the court competences in cases where an entry in the Enterprise Registry is (potentially) wrong. Currently, stakeholders reported that two jurisdictions might apply: parties might need to address both the administrative and the commercial court. This dichotomy of court competences regarding one subject matter raises the question of whether only one court can be identified that is best suited in terms of competence and efficiency.

Three avenues to improve were put forward by business respondents:

- Reducing the number of steps was suggested to improve service delivery.
- Simplifying the process was suggested to improve service delivery.
- Considering providing English language court services was suggested to attract foreign investors.

Some OECD countries have considered introducing English as an optional language for certain types of court proceedings. In Germany, for example, there is an ongoing debate whether the English language should be introduced as an optional language in specific court proceedings. Some courts already offer court proceedings in English (i.e. Landgericht Bonn[35]). Moreover, on the initiative of the Ministry of Justice of Nordrhein-Westfalen, there is a new draft law brought to the Federal Council (*Bundesrat*) to establish specialised chambers in courts for international commerce matters that will conduct court proceedings in English.[36] International chambers of commercial law could be established at selected courts and if both parties agree, the procedural language would be English. The background of this initiative is the experience that large and international disputes are diverted to English courts or arbitration by the parties. Consequently, the local courts are diminished in their relevance. In addition, the substantial court and practitioners' fees generated by such proceedings are lost to another country. Similar initiatives might make sense for public services dealing with foreign investors, such as the Enterprise Registry, the State Land Service and Land Registry offices and the Patent Office.

Financial costs

Several businesses consulted, including surveyed businesses, declared financial costs to be a challenge (4 and 3 out of 11 respondents, respectively).

This result needs to be read in connection with the provision of legal aid. Nine businesses out of ten respondents declared having relied on legal aid to present their case. Legal aid was mostly obtained within one week. The process was found quite difficult.

Moreover, actual or perceived costs of justice borne by businesses may go beyond monetary costs (e.g. court and legal fees). In order to better assess the financial burden of the court service for businesses opportunity costs (e.g. time off work or transportation due to geographic isolation) would need to be taken into account.

Time

Most consulted businesses, both through the interviews and an online survey (8 out of the 11 businesses that responded to the survey on dispute resolution) noted that the main barrier was the time it took for their dispute to settle in court. Moreover, 45% of business respondents further declared it took them more than three months to complete the procedure – from filing an application (5 out of 11 respondents). Some 36% waited between one and three months to meet a judge and almost 55% more than three months (4 and 6 respondents respectively). While most declared it was easy to talk to someone, shorter wait times at walk-in centres and on the phone were suggested to improve service delivery.

During the interviews, opinions were divided. While all stakeholders representing the interests of businesses stressed the significant length of court proceedings, stakeholders representing the government or the court system considered court proceedings to usually be concluded in an acceptable timeframe. The latter added that further improvements are on the way and that delays were rather the responsibility of non-responsive lawyers (electronic calendars might help) and delay tactics by parties (based on rules requiring personal attendance) than due to slow proceedings in court. It was mentioned, however, that some of the very short deadlines (a few days only) applicable to first instance courts were too short and overwhelmed judges in certain situations. When challenging administrative decisions from the Enterprise Registry, delays due to capacity were specifically highlighted, whether before the head of the Register or a court.

Various explanations for these differing perceptions were discussed. Maybe the negative public perception of the duration of court proceedings does not reflect reality, which would lead to the question of how to communicate the speed of services in fact offered. Another explanation could be that the improvements in the duration of proceedings reflected in more recent statistics are due to proceedings that matter less to businesses (for example, private consumer litigation), while those proceedings that matter to businesses might still take a long time.

The Latvian government has undertaken several reforms in this perspective and time savings remains a key focus (Box 3.8). In 2014, amendments to the Civil Procedure Law entered into force, providing an opportunity to transfer a case in proceedings to another court to ensure faster review. Consequently, more than 6 000 cases were transferred from Riga's city courts to other city courts and around 500 cases were transferred from Riga's regional court to other regional courts (Ministry of Justice, 2017). Significant outcomes on the length of judicial proceedings can already be noted, in particular within district courts. Whether it concerns civil, criminal or administrative cases, the duration of proceedings generally decreased. Respectively, the duration went from 9.2 months in 2013 to 7.4 in 2017 (civil cases), from 6.4 months in 2013 to 5.4 in 2017 (criminal cases), and from 13.5 months in 2013 to 7.5 in 2017 (administrative cases). However, it is necessary to also point at lower decrease rates in regional courts of appeal in these three areas. Additionally, the duration in criminal cases marginally increased in regional courts, with proceedings going from 3.5 months in 2013 to 3.7 months in 2017.

Box 3.8. Latvia's action line for better contract enforcement (Extract)

Objective: From 23rd place to 16th in *Doing Business 2019* (with other indicators unchanged), as well as the number of days reduced from 469 to 400 days.

Improvement of monitoring of designated court sittings

The Court Administration proposes to develop the availability of a new e-service for representatives of legal entities, in order to ensure reception of reminders in the user's registered email on designated court sittings in the cases, in which the legal entity whom this person represents is registered in the Court information system as a party to the case.

The plan is to include in the reminder the court name, case number, place and time of the court sitting.

The plan is to provide as a paid CA service the possibility to pre-pay the connection to the service on the portal manas.tiesas.lv, using the payment module of latvija.lv.

The service is aimed at legal entities, who are involved in several judicial proceedings at the same time.

Implementation of the monitoring of data of judicial proceedings, receiving electronic notifications about changes in data of judicial proceedings

The e-service "Monitoring of data of judicial proceedings" receiving electronic notifications about changes in data of judicial proceedings" was introduced to allow a party to any case to obtain information about changes in data of judicial proceedings of the case. The information will be sent to the user's registered email.

The system will prepare an electronic notification on the fact of changes in the information, specifying the possibilities of viewing them on the manas.tiesas.lv portal.

In addition, the plan is to introduce additions, which will provide users with the possibility to pre-pay reception of the service on the portal manas.tiesas.lv, using the payment module of latvija.lv.

Source: Latvia's Court Administration.

The issues of strengthening court efficiency, increasing the number of judges and support of judges by assistants were underscored by stakeholders as decisive factors to reduce the duration of proceedings.[37] To this end, since 2014, the number of judges in Latvia increased by ten in district courts of the Riga judicial region, which handles approximately 40% of civil cases in the country (Ministry of Justice, 2017).

Stakeholders also mentioned their wish for a seamless experience using ICT, e.g. ability to better track their case status.

As in other OECD countries, Latvia is working to improve the use of electronic communication, which has improved significantly in recent times (e.g. introduction of e-files; e-signatures are already accepted). The Appeal Court of Riga, for example, already uses e-cases for specific claims (e.g. disputed statement of an auction of immovable property), and e-signatures for signing documents and parties can file electronically. Everything that the court enters into the court IT system can be seen in a transparent way, also remotely. The Latvian procedural law allows for the sending of electronic communication to parties. Lawyers and prosecutors can only receive electronic communication. Natural persons are still informed by post because the e-address law is not in operation yet (although it can be electronic in cases provided by law). The use of e-ID card could be further explored to optimise the system (Box 3.9).

Box 3.9. Estonia's judicial single computerised system

Launched in 2009 for criminal proceedings, Estonia has a computerised system, common to all judicial actors. Criminal records were incorporated in the system in 2012 and in civil as well as administrative proceedings in 2014.

Electronic communication with court officers and litigants not represented by a lawyer is possible through the system. For lawyers, electronic communication is compulsory, whereas private individuals may choose to use the digitalised system. For anyone who wished to access the computerised platform, the identity card can be used as identification and to file a request, forward papers or documents for the proceedings, and receive procedural acts and judgments in dematerialised form. Access is free. Lawyers, notaries, court clerks, legal representatives and governmental bodies may only communicate with the court by electronic means. Moreover, the portal also allows users to access other useful information systems pertaining to the business register, population register, etc.

Source: Court Quality Framework Design Project (2017).

Latvia has also conducted reforms to improve communication and streamline the process for litigants (Ministry of Justice, 2017). After amendments of the Civil Procedure Law entered into force in early 2017, Latvian courts are now able to communicate with parties electronically via a court informative system, which means receiving court decision and other documents in electronic form. This communication system also became mandatory for sworn advocates. Moreover, the video conferencing system was established in 66 Latvian courtrooms so far, so as to enhance less formal hearing procedures and to lead to more efficient evidence-gathering procedures.

Box 3.10. Communication with the parties: Indicators to measure the quality of the system and communication

Electronic procedures for litigants throughout the proceedings

Depending on the states, electronic communication in proceedings takes different forms and includes different functionalities (filing of claims, and in some systems, management of documents, notification, etc.). This communication may be compulsory in some litigation for professionals, whereas it is optional for private individuals.

Despite the variety of systems and practices, standards have emerged:

- Tools available for all (the parties, their representatives and the courts).
- Minimum technical specifications for electronic communication systems, such as tools' technical capacity for storing, managing and archiving the documents exchanged; a high level of security for the system and exchanges.
- The rate of proceedings covered by the electronic communication system and the rate of procedural acts in different types of litigation (civil, administrative or commercial); it must allow for submitting claims on line, transmitting the necessary documents, and generating automatic notifications for the parties.
- Use of the system must not generate additional costs for litigants.
- System maintenance constitutes a central component of the mechanism's quality (it could rely on the effectiveness of the means introduced, such as dedicated teams inside courts, the management outsourced to private service providers, the existence of assistance for the parties in the event of a system failure).

Indicators should make it possible to evaluate the quality of the system and the communication it allows with the parties:

- The rate of proceedings covered can be measured by counting the number of cases of compulsory and non-compulsory referral by electronic means.
- The coverage rate for procedural acts can be measured by counting the different types of acts that can be performed electronically, where appropriate by litigation type.
- Evaluation of the satisfaction and level of satisfaction for all users (judicial actors, private individuals).
- Regular re-evaluation of the system's capacity. It must lead to corrective measures.

Access to and communication of information for individual cases and proceedings

In addition to the transparency that is necessary for the parties, the foreseeable length of the proceedings and each of their stages represent a key quality management tool for courts. Communication of this information takes the form of a variety of instruments making it possible to provide more or less accurate procedural timeframes:

- standards for the average length of proceedings to predict the length of proceedings
- communication of the timeframe for the proceedings or foreseeable timeframes.

Indicators can help to measure the quality of the mechanisms introduced:

- It is important to measure the systematic nature of the communication of procedural timeframes, procedural timeframes and real-time information on delays.
- The reliability of the information communicated is ensured by:

- comparing the lengths communicated with the effective lengths of the case
- ensuring that average lengths and standards are reviewed regularly and that the corresponding trends are analysed periodically.

- The effectiveness of the means made available to the parties with regard to delays may be measured by counting:
  - the number of claims filed for excessive delays compared to the number of cases pending
  - the proportion of successful claims for excessive delays compared to the total number of claims
  - a qualitative evaluation of the underlying grounds for delays.

Source: Court Quality Framework Design Project (2017).

Specialised processes

Another important issue emphasised by stakeholders during interviews concerned the use of specialised justice.

The specialisation of justice services is a rapidly growing trend in OECD countries according to the legal context of a country. It is utilised as a response to the legal needs of citizens and businesses through service integration for specific legal issues (OECD, 2015e). Different degrees of specialisation exist: from full-fledged court to chamber and internal (informal) tracks (Box 3.11). Judges sitting in court of general jurisdiction may also build or decide to focus their knowledge and expertise on specific matters. This may be said to have a number of advantages, some of which were recognised by Latvian judges. First, greater specialisation allows judges to build expertise in a particular area of law or industry. Secondly, and as a consequence, cases can be reviewed and disposed of more efficiently because the specialised judge may bring her or his knowledge of the species of the dispute to bear upon the proceedings. Thirdly, judicial training can be more focused and help deepen knowledge and expertise, including by assimilating international best practice. Fourthly, the quality of decision making and judgments may improve.

Box 3.11. Specialised bodies and chambers in selected OECD countries

In the United States at the federal level, federal bankruptcy and insolvency courts and handle matters of individual and corporate bankruptcies, and the U.S. Tax Court was notably created to review Internal Revenue Service (IRS) assessments challenged by the taxpayers subject to them. At the state level, the success of Delaware's specialised court of equity (Court of Chancery) in business-related litigation, "the increasing complexity of the commercial world, and growth in the creation and use of complex financial instruments and transaction has prompted a number of states to establish new specialised courts". These include the establishment of a new Commercial Division in New York's state court system, a special Business Court in North Carolina, or a Business Court Division in Nevada's Eight Judicial District.

In France, Commercial Tribunals ("*Tribunaux commerciaux*") have jurisdiction over commercial disputes between businesses and/or corporations and also between businesses and individuals in some circumstances. It also hears bankruptcy matters. Judges are elected traders, "*juges consulaires*" i.e. not career judges. In French Court of Appeals, four chambers are specialised in civil, commercial, criminal and social affairs. The Court of appeal of Paris also have special jurisdiction against decisions from the Competition Council ; Financial Markets Authority ; Regulatory Authority for Electronic Communications and Posts ; Commission for Energy Regulation

In Belgium, commercial tribunals have specialised jurisdiction over petitions linked to postal services, some maritime matters and acts of the national lottery. In Brussels exist French- and a Dutch-speaking tribunal.

In Switzerland, the *Cour de Justice* a second-instance court, is divided into courts of civil, criminal and public law "*Cour civile*"; *Cour pénale*"; "*Cour de droit public*", which are themselves divided into chambers. For instance a specialised chamber under the *Cour civile* hears lease and rent matters. The *Cour pénale* constitutional, administrative and social affairs chambers

In Switzerland, Tribunal des prud'hommes in Swtizerland or Conseils des Tribunal des prud'hommes in Belgium and France hear any disputes concerning work contracts. Employers and employees are both represented in the panels.

In England and Wales, Business and Property Courts were launched in October 2017, acting as an umbrella for specialist financial, business and property litigation and some international civil dispute jurisdictions. It encompasses specialist courts and lists including a Commercial Court, a Business List (with sub-lists on Financial Services and Regulatory oor Pensions), a Competition List; Financial List; Insolvency and Companies List; Intellectual Property List; Property,Trusts and Probate List and Technology and Construction Court. According to the English and Welsh Courts and Tribunals Judiciary, this new arrangement are to "preserve the familiar practices and procedures of these courts, whilst allowing for more flexible cross-deployment of judges with suitable expertise and experience to sit on appropriate business and property cases". Moreover the tribunals system runs alongside the court system and includes a Tax and Chancery Chamber and a Lands Chamber as part of the Upper Tribunal.

Sources: Zimmer, M.B., (2009); Belgium - Ministry of Justice website ; France - Ministry of Justice website; Switzerland - Ministry of Justice website; UK Courts and Tribunal s Judiciary (2017).

This is borne out by the experience (such as it is) in Latvia and internationally. Higher demand for specialised review, backload in court of general jurisdiction or a need for specific technical expertise or to foster business and investment may prompt the implementation of specialised adjudication (OECD, 2016; Kroeze, 2006). Specialised courts, chambers or tracks are seen to be more efficient and effective in the resolution of questions of law, and enhance uniformity and predictability, and improve the quality of judicial decision making. Yet specific challenges exist linked to the preferential selection process or treatment, bias, detachment from the judiciary system and broad judicial knowledge. The experience in England and Wales may be instructive. While more analysis is needed, commercial and business-related specialisation is seen as a tool to attract investments and prevent them from leaving if facing a legal issue (Kroeze, 2006).

Box 3.12. Advantages and risks of establishing judicial specialisation

"Specialisation [...] may have at least three advantages:

- **Greater efficiency**, through specialised procedures, staff and specialised judges who are well versed in the subject matter, which leads to streamlined operations and more efficient processing.
- **Enhanced uniformity**, as a result of dealing with exclusive jurisdiction over particular areas of the law, thereby contributing to greater predictability and confidence in the courts.
- **Quality decisions**, due to greater expertise and experience in applying the law to the facts properly."

"Specialisation may also pose some risks, such as:

- Preferential selection process – may lead to the biased selection of judges and their staff. Circumventing legal requirements in this process may open the door for interest groups to influence the selection process.
- Detachment from the judiciary system – if court specialisation benefits only a small group of court users and positive results and lessons learned are not transferred to other judicial operations. In addition, an important link with the general court system may be lost if their work and education are detached from it.
- A specific group of court users – since judges, lawyers, experts, officials and actors involved in the litigation of cases handled by specialised courts tend to be a small group in each jurisdiction; judges may become familiar with these actors, which may lead to potential preferential treatment or bias in the judges' decisions.
- Less broad experience – through the compartmentalisation of the judges' activity and knowledge of the law, which may stir them away from the knowledge of different areas beyond their own speciality."

Source: Extracts from OECD (2016).

In Latvia the specialisation of judges is currently not very widely spread. The Court House reform gradually consolidates district (city) court areas within the jurisdiction of regional courts, and also introduces specialisation trends.[38] With the consolidation of the smallest jurisdictions, larger courts are established and allows for further specialisation.[39] At the Appeal Court of Riga, for example, all judges are considered to be competent for commercial matters. Yet, a special three-tiered jurisdiction for administrative matters has been in place since 2014. Judicial review related to decisions from the Enterprise Registry and the State Land Service are heard before those administrative courts. As mentioned above, Land Registry Offices are integrated into the district (city) court system.

As mentioned above, Latvia has also introduced specialised tracks in specific areas: Jelgava City Court hears cases related to the decisions of company members (shareholders) meetings; Riga City Vidzeme Suburb Court specialises in cases of industrial property rights (including patents, designs, semiconductor products, trademarks) and hears appeals made against the decision from the Industrial Property Board of Appeal of the Patent Office (Box 3.13). It is worth noting that litigants are represented by specialised patent lawyers in the first and second instances.

Box 3.13. Administrative challenges, patent litigation and enforcement in Latvia

Challenging a decision from the Patent Office

Opposition to the registration of a design and trademark may be submitted in writing (including electronically) to the Patent Office within three months after the receipt of its decision, while opposition to the grant of an appeal from any stakeholder is open until nine months after the publication of the grant of the patent in the Official Gazette. A fee is set for EUR 150 for filing an appeal and EUR 180 for an opposition. Should the new decision of the Patent Office be unsatisfied, the Industrial Property Board of Appeal of the Patent Office (Board of Appeal)[40] will orally hear the petitioner within three months. A written decision is rendered within a month and can be appealed within six months before the court. Patents are appealable directly before the courts.

Litigation and enforcement

Trademark disputes are heard before the Riga City Vidzeme Suburb Court as the court of first instance, the Riga Regional Court as the court of appeal and the Supreme Court as the court of cassation. The Riga Regional Court acts as the Court of first instance for specific cases related to the reestablishment of a patent right (e.g. prior use; infringement patent; grants of a licence, etc.). All trademark matters are examined solely in bench trials by one judge alone (at first instance) or by collegia of three or five judges (in appeal or cassation instance). Criminal proceedings can also be launched.

Latvia ratified the Unified Patent Court Agreement (UPCA) on 11 January 2018. The UPCA is a court common to 25 EU states that have signed the Agreement on the Court.

According to the Patent Law, a claim pertaining to patents can be filed to a court within three years of finding out the rights may have been infringed. As to a dispute regarding the invalidation of a granted patent, a grant of a licence or provisions of a licence contract may be filed to a court throughout the whole period of validity of the patent.

Preliminary injunctions are remedies available to the trademark owner in trademark infringement actions only and are not applicable to cancellation action. In order to improve the quality of the decisions rendered by the Patent Office, the latter has organised training sessions for judicial staff in co-operation with World Intellectual Property Organization (WIPO), the European Union Intellectual Property Office (EUIPO) and the Latvian Judicial Training Centre (LTMC).

The Board of Appeal examines disputes related to the patents, trademarks, designs and topographies of semiconductor products. Members are appointed for a period of three years by the Ministry of Justice, which also determines its number. The panel is composed of at least three members including a patent lawyer and an external expert. Foreign litigants are represented by a professional patent lawyer from Latvia or the European Union. A register of national professional patent lawyers is administered by the Patent Office.

Source: Anohin, V. and V. Osmans (2017); Anohin, V., B. Batrumovics and K. Grishina, (2016).

The Riga District Court in Sigulda adjudicate only civil matters and the Riga City Northern District Court handles cases of illegal transfer of a child across the border or detainment in a foreign country (Ministry of Justice, 2017). Informal specialisation also occurs (e.g. a judge in the Supreme Court being a specialist in commercial law).

There was some lack of clarity about the formal existence of adequate procedural rules for small claims. It seems that small claims procedures are limited in Latvia, notably against decisions from the Board of Appeal for Industrial Property.[41] This refers to a small claims procedure as a simplified procedure to optimise the proceedings, not only a procedure that is based on documents and is transferred to a regular procedure once the other party contradicts.[42] This approach may be interesting to further explore: 2016 data show incoming small claim matters to amount to 13 022 cases.

There was some lack of clarity about the formal existence of adequate procedural rules for small claims. It seems that small claims procedures are limited in Latvia, notably against decisions from the Board of Appeal for Industrial Property.[43] This refers to a small claims procedure as a simplified procedure to optimise the proceedings, not only a procedure that is based on documents and is transferred to a regular procedure once the other party contradicts.[44] This approach may be interesting to further explore: 2016 data show incoming small claim matters to amount to 13 022 cases.

Stakeholders reported welcoming the possibility of exploring deepened judicial specialisations. Business stakeholders mentioned the introduction of specialised judges either by way of specialised courts or through specialised chambers within courts. For instance, appeals against decisions of the Enterprise Registry could be dealt with by a specialised Commercial Court or, at least, by a Commercial Chamber. In addition, it was discussed whether in land registration cases, the civil courts might be better suited than the administrative courts to deal with these challenges. Some institutional stakeholders consider specialisation to potentially conflict with the principle of random distribution of cases. This is considered an important issue for the perception of courts in society.

In terms of practicalities, stakeholders felt that a formal specialisation only made sense for courts with ten judges and more. Combined specialisation is considered as a possibility to also avoid possible shortages in other areas of the Latvian justice system (on the basis that there are relatively low numbers of courts and judges in the country). To this end, a chamber could combine specialisations in business, banking and business insolvency issues. Moreover, it was suggested that chambers specialise in certain areas but could also cover other types of cases on a subsidiary basis.

Box 3.14. Official registry of patent attorneys in OECD countries

The registry of patent attorneys (which implies the examination of candidates and the assignment of the professional name as well as the authorisation to act as a patent attorney) is done by an official body specialised in the field of industrial property protection. In Latvia and Lithuania, the examination of the candidate falls under the competence of their respective Patent Office. In Estonia, it is the responsibility of the Ministry of Economic Affairs and Communication. In Latvia, the Professional Patent Attorney Qualification Examination Commission consists of employees from the Patent Office and representatives from the Latvian Association of Professional Patent Attorneys.

The legal framework for the patent attorneys' profession is practically identical in the three Baltic states where only the patent attorneys who are included on the list of professional patent attorneys are entitled to represent foreign clients before the Patent Office. The candidates who wish to obtain the authorisation either in trademarks, design or inventions can also be authorised in both fields after having completed all examinations.

However, there are some slight differences in the scope of authorisation of patent attorneys' in Baltic countries with respect to the representation of clients before the courts. Indeed, Estonian patent attorneys may represent clients both in civil and administrative proceedings, whereas in Lithuania a lawyer needs to be involved in the proceedings, and jointly with a patent attorney they are the legal representatives of the client. In Latvia, only sworn advocates at Supreme Court can represent clients before the Supreme Court.

In Germany, in order to be able to practice as a patent attorney, it is mandatory to be admitted to the patent bar. Moreover, the German Patent and Trade Mark Office is responsible for the admission of patent attorneys and patent attorney limited liability companies as well as for registering members of the profession from states of the European Economic Area and Switzerland. The Chamber of Patent Attorneys issues admissions certificates to candidates allowing them to practice the profession using the titles *Patentanwältin* and *Patentanwalt*.

Source: Ostrat, J. (n.d.).

With the reorganised judicial map and the establishment of larger courts where higher numbers of judges now sit, judicial specialisation considerations in Latvia are being revisited. Yet a cautious, evidenced-based and thorough approach is needed based on court resources, the needs of all court users, including citizens, as well as mapping the potential risk (Box 3.12). For instance, the small number of commercial-related administrative cases does not in itself call for a specialised unit (Figure 3.20). It would make sense to develop a comprehensive policy for the integrated delivery of dispute resolution services, i.e. including ADR mechanisms (see below). In doing so, disaggregating between the number of civil and commercial cases would be one of the first steps.

Figure 3.20. Proportion of cases challenging a decision from the Enterprise Registry, Patent Office and Land Service compared to the overall number of administrative cases in 2016

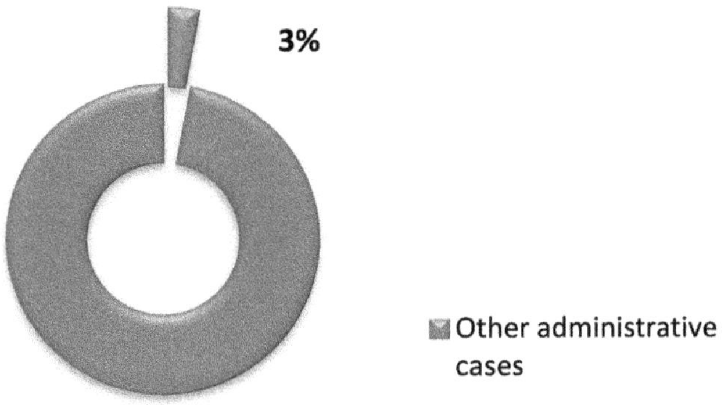

Source: Data from Latvia's Court Administration.

Access to alternative dispute mechanisms in Latvia

Beyond court, there exist different pathways of justice, including contractual compromise, mediation, conciliation, ombudspersons or arbitration. The recent decade saw a new approach to dispute resolution in OECD countries and the European Union. The traditional dichotomy of resolving legal disputes either by way of contractual compromise or by going to court gave way to a more nuanced approach. Multiple avenues can be confusing to some without legal proficiency. The challenge for policy makers is to design a justice ecosystem that helps parties in bringing their dispute to the right forum based on user-centred mechanisms that are fair, effective and efficient. As highlighted during the 2015 OECD Roundtables, "limited co-ordination and lack of a comprehensive approach across justice services are often cited as one of the main challenges in enabling a seamless level of service and access to justice".

Stakeholder interviews in Latvia revealed that there is considerable interest in alternative dispute resolution. Such practice is available in many countries (Box 3.15).

Box 3.15. Examples of commercial alternative dispute resolution mechanisms in OECD countries

Commercial disputes can be resolved outside the public courtroom with alternative dispute resolution mechanisms. Their resolution can take place in arbitral tribunals consisting of one or more arbitrators and parties. The latter are, in principle, free to determine the composition of the tribunal. Arbitral tribunals may be constituted *ad hoc* when parties choose the arbitrators. Arbitrators can also be appointed under the supervision of agencies or organisations directly involved in commercial arbitration.

For instance, in the **United States**, there are several independent and non-profit organisations and agencies that are competent to undertake arbitration in different types of litigation, including commercial litigation. These include the National Academy of Arbitrators (NAA), the American Arbitration Association (AAA), and the Federal Mediation Conciliation Service (FMCS).

Parties can also choose to submit their disputes to specialised bodies such as chambers of commerce. It should be noted that the title of chamber of commerce is applied to somewhat different types of bodies depending on the country. For example, in the

United Kingdom and **Belgium** they are voluntary associations, whose members provide financial resources by subscription. However, they can have a more public status, e.g. in EU member states and in some Latin American countries, where they are bodies whose functions, membership, financial resources, and organisation are prescribed by law.

There are a variety of chambers of commerce in OECD countries. In Germany, the Court of Arbitration of the Hamburg Chamber of Commerce, as an independent institution, conducts arbitration proceedings in domestic and international matters. During the arbitration proceedings, a Legal Counsel from the Chamber of Commerce provides specialised economic and legal advice in the field to parties and arbitrators.

In **Poland**, the Arbitration Court operates at the National Chamber of Commerce of Warsaw. Proceedings before the Arbitration Courts at the NCC are governed by Rules of Arbitration Court at the NCC, which prevail over all non-statutory provisions. The Court is an independent organisational unit consisting of a President, Secretary, Deputy Secretary and arbitrators appointed to hear disputes.

In **Sweden**, commercial disputes through ADR are not resolved directly by the chamber of commerce, but by an institution that is affiliated to it: The Arbitration Institute of the Stockholm Chamber of Commerce. The latter provides dispute resolution services to Swedish and international parties.

Source: US Federal Mediation and Conciliation Service, website; CMS Cameron McKnna (2003); Hamburg Chamber of Commerce, website; Stockholm Chamber of Commerce.

ADR is, however, considered underdeveloped on both sides, i.e. on the side of parties in conflict looking to solve the conflict and on the side of those offering ADR services. These asymmetries, however, reveal different situations for the various ADR mechanisms (see below). While there appear to be gaps in the menu available to Latvian businesses to address their legal issues, stakeholders surveyed do not seem to be fully aware of the potential benefits of a principled approach in choosing the right mechanism for dispute resolution. Between contractual compromise on the one hand and going to court as a form of high escalation on the other hand, businesses interviewed only contemplate arbitration from time to time. Other ways of solving disputes, such as online dispute resolution (Box 3.16), consumer dispute resolution, conciliation, mediation or ombudschemes are currently little considered by businesses, if at all.[45]

Box 3.16. Online dispute resolution services in Latvia

The European Commission Online Dispute Resolution platform approves and lists online disputes resolution providers in EU countries based on "quality standards relating to fairness, efficiency and accessibility" including in Latvia:

Ombudsman for the Latvian Insurers Association deals with complaints on the insurers' decision which allows to undertake insurance business in Latvia on a variety insurance payments for life insurance, assistance insurance, property insurance, insurance for land vehicle and claims pertaining to accident insurance.

Ombudsman of the Association of Latvian Commercial Banks deals with complaints against clearance remittances or transaction through electronic procedures of payment in the framework of the credit institution's activities.

Motor Insurers' Bureau of Latvia ensures that interests of third persons are protected after a traffic accident and promotes security of the mandatory third party liability insurance for persons owning vehicles.

Latvian Council of Sworn Advocates monitors sworn advocates and their assistants in their activities, evaluates complaints against their activities, and is in charge of instigating disciplinary proceedings.

Consumer Rights Protection Centre (Consumer Dispute Resolution Committee) assists consumers to resolve disputes with manufacturers regarding breaches of consumer rights protection regulations submitted by consumers.

Public Utilities Commission incorporates ADR into its processes, as a means of encouraging public participation in the service of public utilities.

Source: European Commission (n.d.); Financial and Capital Market Commission (2011); Motor Insurers' Bureau of Latvia (n.d.); Latvian Council of Sworn Advocates, webpage.

Mediation

Countries offer different types of mediation services under different frameworks and avenues (Figure 3.21). Although differences exist depending on the service providers (i.e. court or private), many countries are grappling with the overall take-up of mediation by their constituency, all the more when this mechanism is not compulsory in the dispute resolution. Fostering the quality, trust and awareness of mediation services is an ongoing process, including in Latvia.

Figure 3.21. The "mediation landscape"

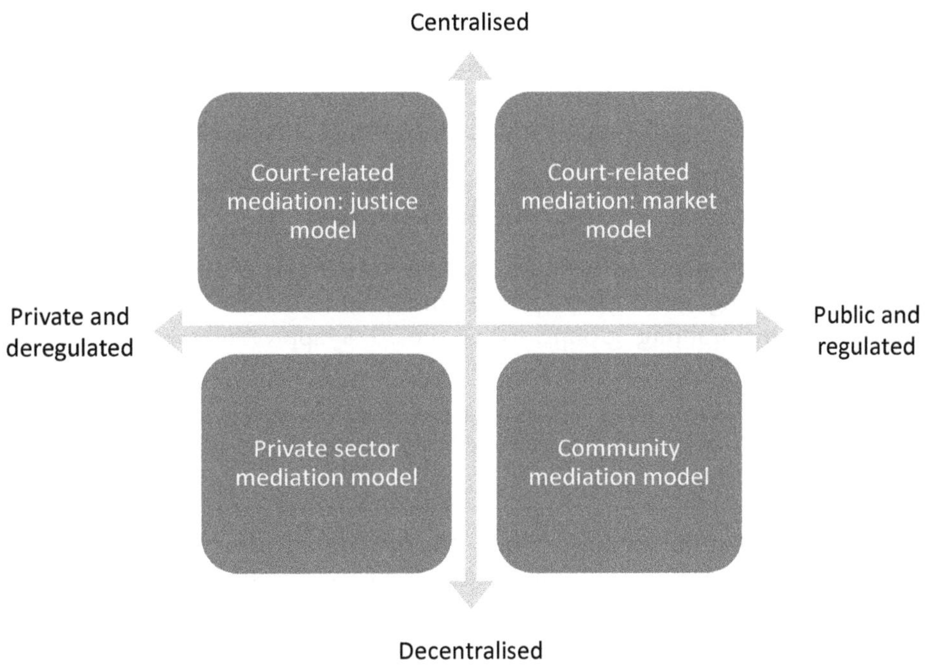

Source: Adapted from International Finance Corporation (2016).

Mediation was introduced in the Latvian legal framework under the Mediation Law of 22 May 2014. Until then mediation services were fragmented and offered sporadically by governmental and non-governmental institutions. The 2014 law establishes the basic principles of mediation, the proceedings, court-annexed mediation and the status of certified mediators. Government-to-business mediation does not exist yet. The Ministry of Finance had been piloting a project to provide mediation services to solve administrative tax issues through mediation.

ADR mechanisms, and in particular mediation, remains estranged from the Latvian dispute resolution culture, despite the fact that stakeholders perceived the process of mediation easier and overall better than going through a traditional court process (seen as more expensive and lengthier). Yet, while there are a number of initiatives underway, mediation for commercial disputes still appears to be underdeveloped in the Latvian context. Latvia is actively looking into ways to promote mediation services (Box 3.17).

Box 3.17. Ongoing efforts to promote mediation services in Latvia

Latvia is aligning itself with recommendations from the European Commission that "Member States should, where necessary and appropriate, increase their efforts to promote and encourage the use of mediation through the various means and mechanisms [...]. In particular, further efforts at the national level should be made to increase the number of cases in which courts invite the parties to use mediation in order to settle their dispute." Authorities believe that in order to promote mediation services, state support is vital, especially since the mediation concept and principles are relatively new. A cultural shift is also needed to change the way people think of conflict resolution.

Several projects are being implemented:

- The first pilot project (launched in 2015) provides a free consultation with a mediator in a number of courts in Riga and courts outside. The consultation is intended for those parties who cannot decide whether or not to agree to the recommendation of mediation as part of a dispute, including commercial ones. The number of courts participating in the project is increasing.
- The second pilot project (2017-18) ensured partial state-funded mediation in family disputes (e.g. five first mediation sessions).
- In 2017-18, in-depth training on mediation issues is provided to judges, court staff, including mediators, and sworn bailiffs. In 2017, nearly 200 people attended the training groups, while in 2018 approximately 350 people are expected.

Source: Information gathered by OECD during stakeholders discussion in March 2018; Commission to the European Parliament and the European Economic and Social Committee (2016).

Court-integrated mediation modules might be considered after evaluating the needs. Initiatives to raise awareness among businesses (e.g. through the confederation of employers) exploring other incentives models (Box 3.18), and to demonstrate the practicalities and cost benefits of mediated solutions should go hand in hand with strengthening the capacity of service providers (e.g. training).

Box 3.18. Current and potential incentive models for Latvia

Current Latvian practice: Repayment of the state fee

The state fee paid by the party to the court is to be repaid back in the amount of 50% from the paid fee if:

- The court approves an amicable agreement between the parties.
- Mediation was successful, certified by a written confirmation from the mediator.

Rights for refund are effective within three years after the state fee is paid into the state budget.

Other potential models

A first regulatory model mediation costs are never borne by the state. It states that a failure to engage and unreasonable refusal to participate in alternative dispute resolution results in cost sanction, i.e. a party culpable is required to cover costs of litigation even if the claim is successful e.g. **United Kingdom**. This incentive holds parties responsible rather than provides financial incentives from the state.

The objective of the second regulatory focuses on court funding by reducing net costs. It aims at weeding out unnecessary court cases. Yet this approach to cost incentive may generate supplementary expenses for the state e.g. Sacramento County, **California**. A grant of US$600 is provided for 3-hour session with a certified mediator.

According to International Finance Corporation (2016), incentive models are seen as advantageous "when the regular costs of mediation are below the regular costs of litigation and arbitration, with no intervention from the state to exert regulatory control". Proposed measures to include: duty for lawyers to discuss alternative dispute resolution options with their clients; mandatory court-connected mediation; subsidy for mediation.

Source: International Finance Corporation (2016).

At present, there is a small number of specialised certified mediators handling a small number of commercial cases in Latvia (Table 3.2).

Table 3.2. Number of certified mediators and commercial cases in Latvia

Mediation and ADR (MADR) (Data for 2012-15) **Certified mediators (CM) (Data for 2015-16)**	2012	2013	2014	2015 Together CM +MADR	2015 (CM)	2016 (CM)
Total number of mediations	299	269	242	272	115	133
Number of mediators who provided data	15	29	29	51	34	38
Commercial cases	**27**	**20**	**20**	**23**	**15**	**11**
Number of commercial mediators	6	6	7	13	10	10

Source: Adapted from Kāpiņa L. (2017).

Some stakeholders think that the courts might be the spark that ADR needs to take root in Latvia (Box 3.19). The role courts play in incentivising parties at early and later stages of court proceedings to consider dispute resolution by ADR mechanisms could indeed be further explored.[46] While measures are being implemented (e.g. dedicated room to mediators recently to give them a physical presence in certain court buildings), court practice was seen as lagging. In terms of lawmaking, some reform of procedural and court organisation reform may be necessary in order to fully equip the courts with the possibility to integrate alternative dispute resolution, based on ongoing initiatives. The introduction of court internal mediation might be a valuable addition in terms of dispute resolution services offered by the court system. Courts could be equipped with an ADR co-ordinator judge who serves as a contact point for both judges internally and parties looking for advice externally.

Box 3.19. Views from certified mediators

Overall, the Ministry of Justice reports establishing positive co-operation with the Council of Certified Mediators to promote mediation services, including through the introduction of pilot projects implemented by the Ministry of Justice with the close co-operation of courts and the Council of Certified Mediators. Yet, the use of mediation remains limited at best. The average number of cases of the certified mediators in Latvia was nine per year. While mediation seems to be recognised to solve family disputes, it is not seen as a relevant dispute resolution mechanism for business matters. Mediators report often feeling limited support for mediation both from state institutions and businesses themselves. Mediators believe that judges and lawyers do not always encourage parties enough to try mediation. The existing pilot projects, e.g. in family law, seem limited to provide the necessary impulses needed for mediation practice, according to them. In fact, there is a view that by only making the first five hours of family mediation free of charge and keeping a very low hourly rate for the following hours of mediators' service, the pilot projects risk sending the signal that mediation is for family, but nor for commercial disputes. Mediators also highlight the need to ensure a competitive and fair service cost.

Mediators reported that their attempts to position mediation as a relevant mechanism for dispute resolution in commercial cases had encountered little interest from the private sector. Feedback from business reflects that there is a predominant need for dispute resolution in the government–to–business area (especially for areas concerning public tenders, construction projects, co-operation between tax administration and businesses regarding the application of the tax issues). State initiatives such as mediation pilot projects in government-to-business disputes were seen by the private sector as controversial and misaligned with the spirit of mediation practice and values.

As mediation is already introduced in the Latvian legal framework and given its strong potential to become an effective and efficient mechanism for business dispute resolution, there is an opportunity to provide the appropriate incentives to use mediation in business disputes or government-to-business disputes (e.g. increased state fee if mediation is not used). This would also require adapting the culture of dispute resolution in Latvia, which still appears to be oriented towards courts and a win-lose mindset. As such, Latvia may strongly benefit from strategic and co-ordinated efforts to enhance public understanding of mediation practice and benefits.

While the introduction of court internal mediation may provide strong opportunities for increasing trust in mediation, its benefits need to be carefully considered with regard to the development of external mediation services. In addition, care should be taken to preserve and develop the skills of professional mediators, which may be at risk in view of the current low demand for service.

Source: Comments from certified mediators, 2018

A number of suggestions were raised (Box 3.20). There could be a mandatory consultation pre-litigation with a mediator (early neutral evaluation). The state fee for proceedings where no mediation was attempted could be increased. Court fees might be reduced if mediation was used. The fees of a certified mediator could be written off for tax obligation purposes. Stricter obligations for lawyers to advise their clients on ADR could be introduced and coupled with documentation duties. Business initiatives could help to makes businesses aware that wrong choices in dispute resolution create costs in their own books.[47]

Box 3.20. Towards an ADR mix for Latvia

Some of the following questions were discussed with mediators as potential ways to improve the position of alternative dispute resolution and mediation, in particular in the mix of Latvian dispute resolution practice:

- Should the Code of Court Procedures be transformed into a Code of Dispute Resolution and cover alternative dispute resolution, such as mediation, and the characteristics of specific procedures?
- Should there be rules on how to transfer from one type of dispute resolution procedure to another?
- Should there be rules on what effects one type of dispute resolution has on another?
- Is there a need to improve the legal effects of mediation?
- Would a way forward be a list of types of disputes in which parties have to try alternative dispute resolution first?
- Should courts be asked to require parties 1) to have a mandatory information session on alternative dispute resolution; and/or 2) to try a specific type of alternative dispute resolution?
- Should the parties to a dispute have an obligation to contact each other before going to court, to discuss alternative dispute resolution and to report the result of these discussions in their court claim statement?
- Should financial state support for alternative dispute resolution be brought into a balance with state support for court proceedings for poor parties?
- What about cost reductions/cost sanctions if alternative dispute resolution is used/not used?

- Are dispute insurances covering alternative dispute resolution? If not, why not?
- Should alternative dispute resolution be made a mandatory subject at university and other places of education?

Latvia may benefit from the continuous reflection process on these questions as it considers ways to strengthen the quality, trustworthiness and take-up of mediation services for business-related disputes.

Arbitration

The use of institutional or ad hoc arbitration services in Latvia was said to be common during the interviews with business. Over recent years Latvia was responsive to the needs of the different stakeholders and is constantly looking to improve its arbitration landscape.

As in many OECD countries, arbitration gained popularity among businesses over a decade ago as a way to expedite the resolution of their disputes. At the time, the court system in Latvia was experiencing heavy backloads that were said to hinder business activities. Consequently, institutional and ad hoc arbitration proliferated: as high as 214 arbitration panels functioned in 2014. It created a perception of "pocket arbitration", lack of quality control and corruption claims in the sentencing and enforcement of awards.

The 2014 Arbitration Law came into force in 2015, which reformed the sector. The law is based on the existing provisions of the Civil Procedure Law at the time and does not follow United Nations Commission on International Trade Law (UNCITRAL) Model Law. It aimed to raise the quality of arbitration in Latvia by increasing the professionalisation of arbitrators, tightening the requirements for accrediting arbitration institutions and embedding fundamental principles to ensure efficient and fair proceedings. Disputes related to employment, trademarks or insolvency procedures as well as involving a state or regional authority or infringing the rights of a third party are excluded. The Enterprise Registry maintains an official online list of arbitration institutions and their rules of procedure. Today, 60 arbitration bodies are active. A party can challenge the validity of an arbitration agreement before the district (city) court as well as request a writ of execution if the award is not complied with voluntarily.

Yet arbitrators remain pessimistic.[48] While it clearly improved the practice, some stakeholders felt it did not go far enough; the 2014 law was seen as dealing with the symptoms rather than the causes (Tipaine and Fjodorova, 2016). The number of arbitration institutions is still deemed too high and offering services at a quality that many stakeholders consider as insufficient. Stakeholders agreed that an ideal number of arbitration institutions in Latvia would be four or five. The enforceability of awards rendered by ad hoc arbitration services is also unclear. When stakeholders summon greater involvement of courts or judicial specialisation in arbitration matters, caution is needed on the impact of court workload.

A ten-year vision was called upon to unlock the use of, and trust in Latvian domestic arbitration. This initiative should be based on a further assessment of the legal needs and experience of stakeholders as well as taking into account the issue of court specialisation in commercial matters (see above).

One way in which the arbitration landscape in Latvia might be rationalised is to consider some process and framework by which arbitration forums and, equally importantly, arbitrators, can receive recognition, or a "stamp of approval".

Conciliation and ombudschemes

The introduction of conciliation and/or ombudschemes, in particular in fields such as banking, insurance and travel might improve business-related dispute resolution. Based on interviews, it seems that such schemes are not very well used. By way of example, the Association of Commercial Banks handled 12 cases in 2014, 8 in 2016 and 6 in 2016. Stakeholders mentioned that the authority of the ombudspersons is limited. Ombudschemes might be provided free of charge to consumers and ombud decisions might have a binding effect for the trader, but not the consumer.[49]

Governance structures and a level playing field for those offering such services require particular attention. Yet further information is needed (e.g. on consumer dispute schemes, for instance) (Box 3.21).

Box 3.21. Drivers of trust in consumer dispute ombudschemes: Views from Germany, France and the United Kingdom

"There [are] different opinions about what builds trust and those responsible for developing public trust in ombudsmen.

The German ombudsmen, retired judges, argued that trust rests with the individual ombudsman concerned. This person is responsible for continually earning the trust of those who approach the ombudsman for help. The independence of the ombudsman is an important factor in building trust.

The French ombudsmen observed that trust was dependent on several factors, the main being speed of decision making, independence, transparency, and neutrality. The importance of avoiding technical jargon and to promote good practices was also noted.

The UK public ombudsman posed the question as to why people do not trust the ombudsmen, suggesting that contributory factors include the context in which they work and how they remedy injustice. They typically deal with complex complaints involving many parties, and a rather extensive process. This context reflects a pre-existing lack of trust in the system.

The private sector ombudsmen argued for the importance of integrity among ombudsmen, and that they should be accessible and provide consumers with a fair and reasonable approach to solving their complaints. It seems that on the one hand consumers are more aware of their rights and are looking for independent help with their complaints, and on the other hand, they seem overwhelmed by the number of pathways available to resolve disputes outside of the courts."

Source: Extract from Hodges, C. *et al.* (2016).

Notes

[1] In March 2018 the Parliament approved upon first reading the amendments identifying eight procedures where the State Land Service is required to send a submission of a land owner to the respective Land Registry Office electronically and vice versa. It provides that changes in one information system should pass to (are entered) another information system within the framework of inter-institutional co-operation.

[2] See also www.simplex.gov.pt/.

[3] The introduction of a national e-ID card was approved by the government in 2010 and a new Personal Identification Documents Law came into force in 2012, defining and regulating the e-ID card types. See Protocol Decision No. 60 on "Possible financing solutions for providing certification services in Identity Cards (e-IDs) and their unique and priority means to ensure electronic identity of individuals" of 8 November 2018, available at http://polsis.mk.gov.lv/documents/5755.

[4] The government acknowledges that in order for the user to technically use the e-ID as an identification tool, it is necessary to make adjustments and install specific units on the user's computer, including card reader drivers; dedicated drivers; and also an additional card-specific integration module to ensure compatibility with specific web browsers and operating systems. For more information, see the Informative Report on "Possible financing solutions for providing certification services in Identity Cards (e-IDs) and their unique and priority means to ensure electronic identity of individuals", of 8 November 2018, available at http://polsis.mk.gov.lv/documents/5755.

[5] Based on EU Directive 2012/17/EU and EU Regulation 2015/884.

[6] The law is available at https://likumi.lv/doc.php?id=72847&version_date=08.04.2009.

[7] Signatures can also be certified by sworn notaries or using e-signatures.

[8] For a description of the registration procedures, see Chapter 3.

[9] Information provided by the Ministry of Economy.

[10] Latvia highlighted that the 324 private limited companies and 1 public limited company were set up in 2016 and founders were Latvian citizen or Latvian companies; compared to 10 320 new limited companies in Latvia.

[11] Some data quality checks are performed by the Enterprise Registry, for instance information about natural persons are checked in the Population Register, addresses in the State Addresses Register, and information about property in the Land Registry.

[12] It is worth noting that the Enterprise Registry does not have jurisdiction to examine private agreements of shareholders (stakeholders) included in the articles of association in accordance with Article 144 Paragraph 1 Point 8 and 9 of the Commercial Law.

[13] Information provided by the Ministry of Economy. Information provided by the Ministry of Economy.

[14] Users may be interested in knowing two different things: 1) the complete and up-to-date information on the register regarding a certain business entity; 2) only the amendments concerning a business entity for a recent time period. In the second point, the user does not want to see the entire information, but is only interested in the particular elements that have been changed in a specific time period.

[15] "The entries in the Enterprise Registry shall be published by the court, sorted by days and in the chronological order of their entry, in the electronic information and communication system designated by the *Land* department of justice [...]. Unless the law provides otherwise, the entries shall be notified in their entirety."

[16] Information provided by the Ministry of Economy.

[17] Information provided by the Ministry of Economy.

[18] Latvia highlights that it is not possible to submit documents via email if the service is available on the e-platform, according to amendments of the law "On the Enterprise Registry of the Republic of Latvia" (1 May 2017).

[19] The Cabinet determines the list of the state authorities and officials (courts, public authorities, notaries, bailiffs and others authorities) to whom the holder of the Computerised Land Registry will provide the information. For others, the information is provided under the permission of the Head of the Land Registry Office if the information is necessary for the protection of infringed or contested rights of such persons or their interests protected by law.

[20] Accordance with Land Registry Law, Art. 132 - Prior to the certification of such transactions, the object of which are rights entered or to be entered in a Land Registry, as well as prior to the certification of a request for confirmation, a notary has a duty to examine the relevant division of the Computerised Land Registry. The process to verify the title of the real estate and real rights are not obligatory.

[21] Information provided by the Ministry of Economy.

[22] As previously mentioned, in March 2018 the Parliament approved in the first reading the amendments, identifying eight procedures where the State Land Service must send a submission of a land owner to the respective Land Registry Office electronically and vice versa. It provides that changes in one information system pass to (are entered) in another information system within the framework of inter-institutional co-operation. Sworn notaries will also have to electronically submit a request for corroboration to the Land Registry office as well as when it deals with mortgages.

[23] "The sub-par patenting system may have contributed to the low research and innovation spending, particularly in the public sector"; see OECD (2015c).

[24] A total of 295 businesses representatives participated in the overall survey on access to business justice services with 62 responding to the legal needs and experience section. These data should be interpreted with caution. The survey was disseminated by the Court Administration and promoted through various governmental and business websites. Interviews with business stakeholders during two fact-finding missions (July and October 2017), information received from Latvia and desk research also contributed to the findings in this chapter.

[25] Productivity Commission (2015) in Pleasence and Balmer (2017b).

[26] Engelmann and Cornell (1988), Bhagat, Brickley and Coles (1994), and Bhagat, Bizjak and Coles (1998) in Bhagat and Romano (2001).

[27] This was a small sample size.

[28] See also van der Horst, de Vree and van der Zeijden (2006).

[29] For example, see IPO (2010).

[30] See Pleasence and Balmer (2017a).

[31] See Pleasence and Balmer (2013) in Pleasence and Balmer (2017a).

32 The main goals of the reform were to: 1) reduce and prevent unequal caseload distribution among courts; 2) ensure random distribution of cases; 3) enhance the specialisation of judges; 4) increase the overall quality of court rulings and of judicial services; 5) reduce the length of proceedings; 6) optimise the allocation of court resources.

33 The scope of the review encompasses disputes arising from public procurement processes.

34 See the Strategy of Activity of the Supreme Court of the Republic of Latvia 2017-2019.

35 See www.lg-bonn.nrw.de/behoerde/englischsprachige-zk/index.php (in German).

36 See www.justiz.nrw.de/Mitteilungen/2018_03_02_Wirtschaftsprozesse_auf_Englisch/index.php (in German).

37 Information gathered by the OECD during the OECD fact-finding mission, July 2017.

38 Prior to the Court House reform, it was difficult for a judge to specialise due to the small size of most of the district (city) court (authorities). Latvia had a wide network of small first instance courts. Some 65% of all district (city) courts had fewer than 7 judges (3-7 judges) in a court. Some 26% of district (city) courts had 8-14 judges in court, and there were only 3 district (city) courts with more than 14 judges (Authorities).

39 The Chief Judge of a court prior to the beginning of each calendar year establishes a list of specialisations within the court. He or she will consider the organisation of the district (city) court, work experience and the specific knowledge of a judge. Specialisation occurs only if it is possible to ensure the random distribution of cases, according to the Law on Judicial Power (Authorities).

40 Chapter 30.3, Civil Procedure Law.

41 Chapter 30.3, Civil Procedure Law.

42 Information gathered by the OECD during the OECD fact-finding mission, July 2017.

43 Chapter 30.3, Civil Procedure Law.

44 Information gathered by the OECD during the OECD fact-finding mission, July 2017.

45 Information gathered by the OECD from government sources during the OECD fact-finding mission, July 2017.

46 Information gathered by the OECD during the OECD fact-finding mission, July 2017.

47 Information gathered by the OECD during the OECD fact-finding mission, July 2017.

48 Information gathered by the OECD during the OECD fact-finding mission, July 2017.

49 Information gathered by the OECD during the OECD fact-finding mission, July 2017.

References

Anohin, V. and V. Osmans (2017), "Patents 2018: Latvia", International Comparative Legal Guides.

Anohin, V., B. Batrumovics and K. Grishina, (2016), "Litigation procedures and strategies: Latvia", World Trademark Review, 13 December 2016.

Australia - Attorney-General's Department (2009), A Strategic Framework for Access to Justice in the Federal Civil Justice System, A guide for future action, Access to Justice Taskforce.

Australia - Department for Industry, Innovation and Science website.

Austria - Unternehmensserviceportal, www.usp.gv.at/Portal.Node/usp/public.

Baltic Legal (n.d.), "Register of Enterprises of Latvia: a place to register a company", webpage, www.baltic-legal.com/commercial-register-of-latvia-eng.htm (accessed 11 May 2018).

Belgium - Ministry of Justice website https://www.tribunaux-rechtbanken.be/fr/tribunaux-cours/tribunal-de-commerce.

Bhagat, S. and R. Romano, (2001), "Event Studies and the Law--Part I: Technique and Corporate Litigation", *John M. Olin Center for Studies in Law, Economics, and Public Policy Working Papers*, Paper 259.

Blackburn, R., J. Kitching and G. Saridakis (2015), "The legal needs of small businesses: An analysis of small businesses' experience of legal problems, capacity and attitudes", Small Business Research Centre, for the Legal Services Board, Kingston University.

Business Register of Estonia (2017), "Efficient e-governance in practice: Centre of Registers and Information Systems and e-Business Register of Estonia", presentation, March.

CEPEJ (2018), "Evaluation of the Latvian Judicial system on the basis of the methodology and tools developed by the CEPEJ", CEPEJ-COOP(2018)1, March 2018, https://www.ta.gov.lv/UserFiles/Faili/CEPEJ_Evaluation_Report_Latvia_Final_En.pdf.

Chile - "Tu Empresa en Un Día" (2017), Monthly report on businesses and societies creation , May; www.empresasenundia.cl/wp-content/uploads/2015/08/Informe-RES-Mayo-2017.pdf.

CMS Cameron McKnna (2003) "Polish Business Law", in Zdzislaw Brodecki (ed.), The Hague, Kluwer Law International.

Commission to the European Parliament and the European Economic and Social Committee (2016), Report on the application of Directive 2008/52/EC of the European Parliament and of the Council on certain aspects of mediation in civil and commercial matters (COM [2016] 542 final).

Court Quality Framework Design Project (CQFD) (2017), "Handbook on Quality of Justice".

e-Governance Academy (n.d.), "e-Business is awesome", https://ria.ee/public/publikatsioonid/e-Business_demo.pdf (accessed 11 May 2018).

Estonia - Business Register (2017), "Efficient e-governance in practice: Centre of Registers and Information Systems and e-Business Register of Estonia", presentation, March 2017 (updated).

Estonia - E-residency website, https://e-resident.gov.ee/.

European Commerce Registers Forum (2016), "2016 International Business Registers Report", www.ecrforum.org/wp-content/uploads/2016/05/IBRR_2016_webb.pdf (accessed 30 January 2018).

European Commission (2015), "Quality of Public Administration - A Toolbox for Practitioners", European Social Fund, http://ec.europa.eu/esf/main.jsp?catId=3&langId=en&keywords=&langSel=&pubType=434.

European Commission (n.d.), "Online dispute resolution", webpage, https://ec.europa.eu/consumers/odr/main/?event=main.adr.show2 (accessed 11 May 2018).

European e-Justice (2016), "Land registers in Member States – Latvia", webpage, https://e-justice.europa.eu/content_land_registers_in_member_states-109-lv-en.do?member=1 (accessed 11 May 2018).

European e-Justice (2015), "Land registers in Member States – Germany", webpage, https://e-justice.europa.eu/content_land_registers_in_member_states-109-de-en.do?member=1 (accessed 11 May 2018).

European Trade Mark and Design Network website, https://euipo.europa.eu/ohimportal/en/european-trade-mark-and-design-network.

Financial and Capital Market Commission (2011), "Consumer complaints handling and settlement of disputes regarding financial services within the authority of FCMC and other institutions", www.fktk.lv/en/commission/about-us/2011-10-19-consumer-complaints-hand.html.

France - Ministry of Justice website http://www.justice.gouv.fr/organisation-de-la-justice-10031/lordre-judiciaire-10033/tribunal-de-commerce-12031.html.

Gencs Valters Law Firm (2016), "Patent registration in Latvia", webpage, www.gencs.eu/news/index/839 (accessed 11 May 2018).

Gómez, Manuel A. (2008), "All in the Family: The Influence of Social Networks on Dispute Processing (A Case Study of a Developing Economy)", 36 *GA. J. INT'L & COMP. L.* 291.

Hodges, C. et al. (2016), "ADR and Justice in Consumer Disputes in the EU", *Policy Brief*, Foundation for Law, Justice and Society, www.fljs.org/sites/www.fljs.org/files/publications/ADRandJustice%20Rev%202.pdf (accessed 11 May 2018).

International Finance Corporation (2016), "Making Mediation Law", *Mediation Series*, http://documents.worldbank.org/curated/en/899611503551941578/pdf/119067-WP-REV-11-9-2017-15-33-48-MakingMedLaw.pdf.

Intellectual Property Office (IPO) (2010), "Intellectual Property Enforcement in Smaller UK Firms", Report for the Strategy Advisory Board for Intellectual Property Policy (SABIP), Greenhalgh, C. et al., 1 October 2010.

Kāpiņa L. (2017), "Balance of Diving and Interception in Commercial Dispute Mediation: Latvian Mediators' Experience and Opinions", prepared in the framework of the conference "Mediation - Achievements and Challenges", May.

Kroeze M. J. (2006), "The Dutch Companies and Business Court as a Specialized Court" in "The Quality of Corporate Law and the Role of Corporate Law Judges", Bouchez L., Knubben M., McCahery J. A. & Timmerman L. (eds), Amsterdam Centre for Corporate Finance.

Latvia - Ministry of Justice website. www.tm.gov.lv/en/ministry/authorities.

Latvian Council of Sworn Advocates, webpage, www.advokatura.lv/en/council/ (accessed 11 May 2018).

Lupo G. and Bailey J. (2014), "Designing and Implementing e-Justice Systems: Some Lessons Learned from EU and Canadian Examples", Laws, Vol. 3, No., 24 June 2014.

Ministry of Justice (2017), "Role in Judicial System", Republic of Latvia.

Motor Insurers' Bureau of Latvia (n.d.), "About us", webpage, www.ltab.lv/en/about-us/mib/ (accessed 11 May 2018).

Netherland - Ministry of Safety and Justice website.

Norton Rose Fulbright (2017), Litigation Trends Annual Survey, http://www.nortonrosefulbright.com/knowledge/publications/142155/2016-litigation-trends-annual-survey.

Norway - Brønnøysund Register Centre website, https://www.brreg.no/home/.

OECD (2017a), Legal needs and experience - Questionnaire for Businesses.

OECD (2017b), "OECD Policy Roundtable on Equal Access to Justice", Session notes, OECD Conference Centre, 22-23 May 2017, Paris.

http://www.oecd.org/gov/A2J-RT-Session-notes-May-2017.pdf.

OECD (2016), *The resolution of competition cases by specialised and generalist courts: Stocktaking of international experiences,* www.oecd.org/daf/competition/The-resolution-of-competition-cases-by-Specialised-and-Generalist-Courts-2016.pdf.

OECD (2015a), *Government at a Glance 2015*, OECD Publishing, Paris, http://dx.doi.org/10.1787/gov_glance-2015-en.

OECD (2015b), *Global Forum on Transparency and Exchange of Information for Tax Purposes Peer Reviews: Latvia 2015: Phase 2: Implementation of the Standard in Practice*, OECD Publishing, Paris, http://dx.doi.org/10.1787/9789264245068-en.

OECD (2015c), *OECD Economic Surveys: Latvia 2015*, OECD Publishing, Paris, http://dx.doi.org/10.1787/9789264228467-en.

OECD (2015d), *Equal Access to Justice, OECD Expert Roundtable, Background notes,* 7 October 2015, www.oecd.org/gov/Equal-Access-Justice-Roundtable-background-note.pdf.

OECD (2015e), *Equal Access to Justice, OECD 2nd Expert Roundtable, Background notes,* 1 December 2015, www.oecd.org/gov/Equal-Access-Justice-Roundtable2-background-note.pdf.

OECD (2010a), *Better Regulation in Europe: Portugal 2010*, OECD Publishing, Paris, http://dx.doi.org/10.1787/9789264084575-en.

OECD (2010b), *Competitiveness and Private Sector Development: Egypt 2010: Business Climate Development Strategy*, OECD Publishing, Paris, http://dx.doi.org/10.1787/9789264087408-en.

OECD (2009), *Tuempresa.gob.mx: A One-Stop Shop for Quick and Easy Business Start-Ups in Mexico*, www.oecd.org/dataoecd/55/36/43863212.pdf.

OECD (2003), *From Red Tape to Smart Tape: Administrative Simplification in OECD Countries*, OECD Publishing, Paris, http://dx.doi.org/10.1787/9789264100688-en.

ORIMA Research (2010), "Small Business Dispute Resolution", Summary Report, Department of Innovation, Industry, Science and Research (DIISR), Industry and Business Policy Division, June 2010 https://industry.gov.au/smallbusiness/asbfeo/Documents/DisputeResolutionSurveyReport.pdf.

Ostrat, J. (n.d.), "Patent litigation in the Baltic states: Estonia, Latvia and Lithuania", www.lasvet.ee/est/g22s46 (accessed 11 May 2018).

Pleasence, P. and N.J. Balmer (2017a), "It's personal: Business ownership and the experience of legal problems", *Justice Issues*, Paper 24, November.

Pleasence, P. and N.J. Balmer (2017b), "From the frying pan to the fire: The impact of small businesses' legal problems", *Justice Issues*, No. 52, June.

Pleasence, P. and N.J. Balmer (2013), *In Need of Advice? Findings of a Small Business Legal Needs Benchmarking Survey*, Legal Services Board, Cambridge, April 2013.

Strasburger, L. (1999), "The Litigant-Patient: Mental Health Consequences of Civil Litigation", *Journal of the American Academy of Psychiatry Law*, Vol. 27, No. 2, pp. 203-11.

Stockholm Chamber of Commerce, Arbitration Institute website: www.sccinstitute.com/dispute-resolution/.

Switzerland - Ministry of Justice website: http://ge.ch/justice/tribunal-des-prudhommes.

TexasOnline-eFiling for courts (2005), "Electronic Document Filing", website: https://www.texasonline.state.tx.us/downloadables/apps/efiling/caseStudyv6.pdf .

Tipaine, M. and L. Fjodorova (25 January 2016), "Arbitration in Latvia: Was a Restart a Failure?", *Kluwer Arbitration Blog.*

UK Courts and Tribunal s Judiciary (2017), Advisory note, October 2017 https://www.judiciary.gov.uk/wp-content/uploads/2017/09/bpc-advisory-note-13-oct2017.pdf ; https://www.judiciary.gov.uk/about-the-judiciary/the-justice-system/court-structure/.

US Chamber litigation, website: www.chamberlitigation.com/who-we-are.

US Federal Mediation and Conciliation Service, Arbitration Policies and Procedures, Code of Federal Regulation Alternative Dispute Resolution, 29 CFR PART 1404—Arbitration Services, website: www.fmcs.gov/services/arbitration/arbitration-policies-and-procedures/

van der Horst, R., R. de Vree and P. van der Zeijden (2006), "SME Access to Alternative Dispute Resolution Systems", EIM Business and Policy Research.

World Bank (2015), *Registering Property: Measuring the Quality of Land Administration Systems*, World Bank, Washington, DC.

World Bank (2014), *Improving Court Efficiency, the Republic of Korea's e-Court Experience*, World Bank, Washington, DC.

Zimmer, M.B., Overview of Specialized Courts (January 9, 2017). International Journal for Court Administration, Vol. 2, No. 1, 2009.

Chapter 4. Measuring the administrative costs of starting a business in Latvia

This chapter seeks to measure administrative costs related to selected procedures prescribed under the Commercial Law. It identifies and analyses possible simplification measures that may support the starting-up or re-organisation of business operations and translate into cost savings. The main focus of this chapter is put on reducing administrative burden generated from selected business registration procedures administered by the Latvian Enterprise Registry, i.e. registrations of an individual merchant and a limited liability company with decreased capital, and reorganisation of a limited liability company through merger by acquisition. The chapter presents evidence that may be considered to substantiate legal amendments and changes in procedural practice and make the relationship with businesses more efficient, as presented in Chapter 1.

Identifying and managing the costs that regulations impose on businesses is at the core of many initiatives by OECD countries to improve regulatory quality, particularly when governments seek to make the domestic business environment more competitive and attractive for economic activity, ensuring a fair level playing field for all companies. As the previous chapter highlighted, Latvia is no exception to this trend and over the last few years efforts have been made to introduce simplification measures to help business operations. The diffusion of information and communication technology (ICT) and e-government solutions contributed to greater clarity, transparency and efficiency of the relationship with state institutions, but challenges remain. Because it is the main legal instrument for doing business in Latvia, this chapter focuses on the Commercial Law.

In particular, this chapter seeks to measure the administrative costs related to selected procedures provided for by the Commercial Law and to identify possible simplification measures that may translate into cost savings for businesses. By doing so, evidence is presented that may be considered to substantiate legal amendments and make the relationship with businesses more efficient (for the methodology, see Annex 3.A).

In order to continue the pattern of reforms and with a view to meet the government target of placing Latvia among the leading countries in both the World Bank Doing Business Index and the World Economic Forum Global Competitiveness Index, the Latvian Ministry of Justice identified three formalities regulated by the Commercial Law for which there might be margin for improvement, and for designing possible simplification measures on the basis of a quantification of the related administrative costs (Box 4.1).

Box 4.1. Selected formalities in the OECD cost assessment

The OECD measurement covers three procedures performed by businesses when interacting with the Enterprise Registry of Latvia. They are:

- the registration of an individual merchant (individuā lais komersants, IK)
- the registration of a limited liability company with decreased equity capital of EUR 2 800 or below (sabiedrība ar ierobež otu atbildību, SIA)
- the reorganisation of a limited liability company, through merger by acquisition.

All three procedures are managed by the Latvian Enterprise Registry, which is also responsible for implementing the legal amendments and the simplification measures affecting them.

Starting a business in Latvia is not confined to the sheer registration procedure that entrepreneurs have to follow at the Latvian Enterprise Registry. The main task of the Registry is to ensure the company has a valid legal name and legal address, while the rest of the authorisations needed to operate are managed by other authorities, such as the State Revenue Service and the various institutions responsible for licenses to operate. Besides intervening at the very outset of the procedure, nonetheless, the Enterprise Registry plays a pivotal role since it is the institution where all modifications to the statute and organisation of companies have to be notified by businesses.

Focus: Reducing administrative burden for business registration

Registration of an individual merchant

The definition and registration of an individual merchant are regulated in Part B, Division VIII of the Commercial Law of Latvia. According to Section 74 therein, "an individual merchant is a natural person who is registered as a merchant with the Enterprise Registry."

The application to the Enterprise Registry to register as an individual merchant entails a series of administrative activities, of which some are out of the scope of the registration process at the Registry itself, but they are necessary to complete the registration. In particular, applicants have to provide the name they selected for their firm. Even if the Registry offers the possibility to check if that name is available and may be used (a procedure that can take up to three days if done by a state notary at the Registry), the applicants can do their own search on various websites – including the website of the Enterprise Registry where this information is available free of charge - to make sure the name is available.

Applicants must then fill in some forms that the Enterprise Registry has tried to simplify (making them short and user-friendly). In some cases, the Registry has also published guidelines to facilitate this process, guiding the user on what type of information has to be inserted in the required fields.

The information to be included in the application dossier is rather minimal. It consists of the personal data (name, surname), the chosen name of the legal entity and a legal address. As to the latter, the applicant has to include a written consent by the owner of the property, if he or she does not personally own the physical place where the business will be registered.

Online registration is possible. Nonetheless, registrations of individual merchants continue to be a process mainly carried out in person. This holds also for the step of notarising signatures, which may take place at the Registry's venue by scheduling an appointment with a state notary, if the applicant prefers to do so instead of recurring to a sworn notary. The comparatively limited use of e-signatures in Latvia has reduced the possibility of making the procedure completely online-only (see Chapter 2 for further information on access to the Enterprise Registry).

The visit to the Enterprise Registry is relatively short, and if all data and additional requirements are complete and correct, then the file is admitted. Before leaving, the future individual merchant has to make the necessary payments, unless payments were made beforehand, directly at a bank, in which case the applicant must show the corresponding receipts. The costs amount to EUR 30 for the firm registration and EUR 18.50 for the future publication of the registration in the Official Gazette.

The Enterprise Registry then performs a series of checks in order to verify the information provided by the user is correct. In particular, the issue of the legal address is relevant and is cross-checked with other registries (such as the Land Registry and cadastre) to ensure the address is valid and that there is no risk of irregularities. The checks can last from one to three days, when the Enterprise Registry informs the individual merchant either by email, post or in person. In the case of a refusal, the Enterprise Registry sends a priority letter or email to the legal address explaining the reasons for the negative response.

Table 4.1sums up the activities required to register an individual merchant, indicating the associated time and costs.

Table 4.1. Activities, time required and associated fees to register an individual merchant in the Enterprise Registry

Activities	Time and costs associated
1. Gather information on the process and requirements to be presented	180 minutes
2. Download the forms to be filled in	15 minutes
3. Ask for an appointment with the state notary	24 hours
4. Visit the Enterprise Registry, submit application and forms and make the payments	60 minutes (travel) + EUR 10 (transport) + 30 minutes (at the Enterprise Registry) + EUR 61.50 (fees)
5. Receive the positive notification	72 hours

Source: Author.

The administrative costs for an individual merchant to conduct this procedure amount to EUR 369 and it takes 4.6 days to complete the whole procedure to register an individual merchant. In 2016, 603 individual merchants were registered in the Enterprise Registry of Latvia, and the total administrative costs of those people to comply with the process amounted to EUR 222 508.65. The main administrative costs and administrative activities are shown in Figure 4.1.

Figure 4.1. Administrative activities and costs of the registration of an individual merchant

In EUR and as % of the total cost

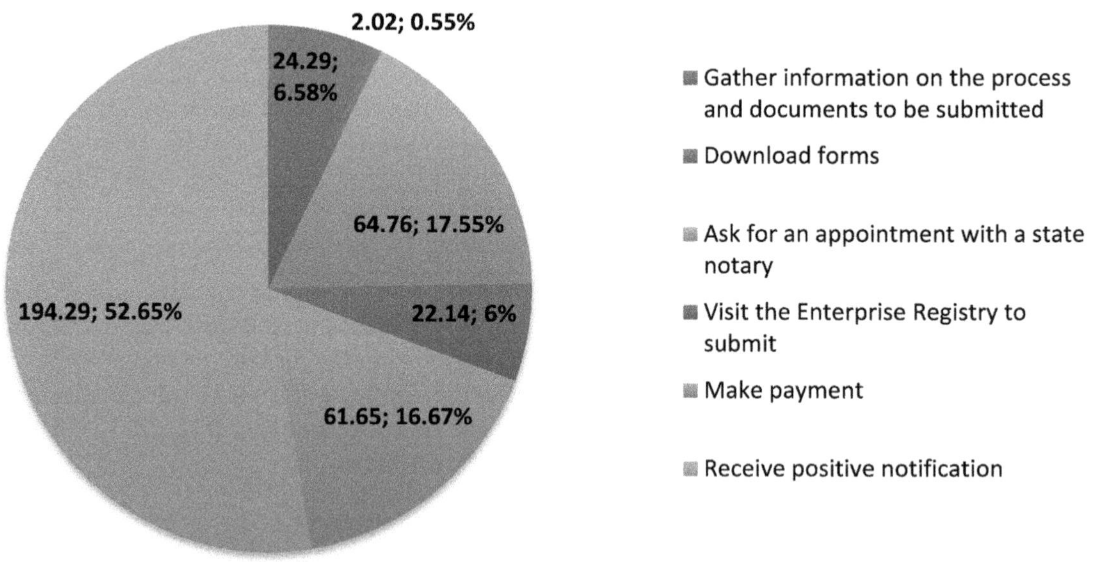

Source: Author.

In this procedure, the estimated waiting time related to the notification of the decision by the Enterprise Registry accounts for 52.65% of the total administrative cost, while the visit to the notary (17.55% of the total administrative cost) and the visit to the Enterprise Registry to hand in the application dossier and make the payments (6% of the total administrative costs), also increase the time that businesses have to invest when dealing with institutions and waiting for their reactions.

Registration of a limited liability company with decreased capital

Division IX on "Capital Companies" in Chapter 1 of the Commercial Law defines a limited liability company (LLC) and Chapter 2 describes its registration procedure in the Enterprise Registry.

Provisions pertaining to a so-called "LLC with decreased capital" are specified in Section 185(1) of the law, which spells out "Special Provisions in Relation the Amount of the Equity Capital". The section establishes that upon compliance with certain conditions, a minimum equity capital of less than EUR 2 800 can be accepted for such a type of company. The conditions include:

- The founders and the shareholders of the company are natural persons and there can only be up to five of them.
- Each shareholder of the company is a shareholder of only one such LLC.
- The board of directors of the company consists of one or several members, and they all are shareholders of the company.
- Other conditions related to the equity capital of the company.

At present, LLCs with decreased capital are quite common in Latvia, to the point that many individual entrepreneurs prefer to register as a limited liability company with decreased capital instead of as an individual merchant.

The procedure to register an LLC with decreased capital is quite similar to the one pertaining to the individual merchant, the main difference being the larger number of documents that have to be presented. Also in this case, written consent from the owner has to be attached to the application file if the legal address, understood as the address where the management of the company (headquarters of the company) is located, is not owned by the company. The cadastre number of the immovable property, the given name, surname and personal identification number or name (firm name) and registration number of the owner shall be indicated in the consent.

In addition, a number of documents related to the company have to be presented, including: the application form, the decision to found an LLC, the statute of the company, the shareholder distribution, the board announcement of the legal address, and the consent of the real estate owner.

In some cases, these documents can be easily produced by the applicants – the Enterprise Registry does not mandate using any particular format, merely requiring that the correct information is properly submitted. Guidelines and examples are published on the website of the Enterprise Registry, which can help applicants prepare such documents, in case they do not have the professional support of a lawyer or accountant.

The following payments are related to this procedure: EUR 20 state tax for registration; EUR 14.23 for the publication in the Official Gazette; and EUR 9 for each notarised signature. If the procedure is done on line, a 10% discount on the price of the state tax applies. This requires the use of the e-signature by all shareholders of the company.

Once the application dossier is submitted to the Enterprise Registry, the latter proceeds to several checks. The task normally lasts up to three working days. If the applicant wants the check to be performed under a fast-track procedure, an additional payment of EUR 60 is charged by the Registry.

Table 4.2 lists the activities that the procedure entails, as well as the time and costs related to them.

Table 4.2. Activities, time required and associated fees to register a limited liability company with decreased capital in the Enterprise Registry

Activities	Time and costs associated
1. Gather information on the process and requirements to be presented	180 minutes
2. Download the forms to be filled in	15 minutes
3. Compile the list of documents to be presented:	24 hours + EUR 50 (for a lawyer)
3.1. Application form	-
3.2. Decision to found a limited liability company	-
3.3. Statute of the company	-
3.4. Shareholder distribution with notarised signature	-
3.5. Board announcement of the legal address	-
3.6. If necessary, agreement of the real estate owner	-
4. Ask for an appointment with the state notary	24 hours
5. Visit the Enterprise Registry, submit application and forms and make the payments	60 minutes (travel) + EUR 10 (transport) + 30 minutes (at the Enterprise Registry) + EUR 56.23 (fees)
6. Receive the positive notification	72 hours

Source: Author.

The administrative costs associated with the registration of an LLC with decreased capital amount to the equivalent of EUR 478.49. It takes around 5.6 days for applicants to complete the whole process with the Enterprise Registry.

In 2016, a total of 10 316 companies of this type received a positive notification from the Enterprise Registry, meaning that the total administrative costs associated with this procedure were EUR 4 936 117.35, an equivalent of 0.019% of Latvia's GDP. The main costs related to this procedure are presented in Figure 4.1, in relation to the various activities that have to be undertaken to complete the registration with the Enterprise Registry.

Figure 4.2. Administrative activities and costs of the registration of a limited liability company with decreased capital

In EUR and as % of the total cost

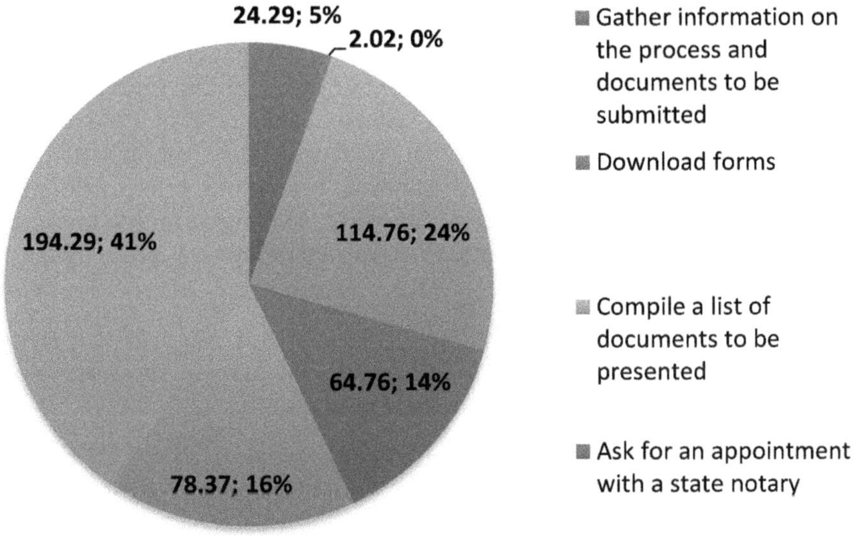

Source: Author.

As it can be observed, the main source of cost (41% of the total administrative costs) is associated with the final stage of the process, when the applicant needs to wait for three days to receive the positive notification. Activities such as compiling the necessary information (24% of the total administrative cost) and scheduling an appointment with the state notary at the Registry (14% of the total administrative cost) also imply some waiting time.

In total, businesses spend around 57% of the whole process waiting for responses from third parties, being the Enterprise Registry or other experts required to provide the requested information.

Reorganisation of a limited liability company through merger by acquisition

Part C of the Commercial Law describes the different forms in which a commercial company can be reorganised, either by merging, division or by restructuring. Section 335 establishes the different forms of merging. The procedure that was mapped and measured by the OECD is an acquisition, which is defined as "a process in which a company (the acquired company) transfers all of its property to another company (the acquiring company)." The Enterprise Registry must be notified of the decision to merge companies.

The procedure consists of two stages. The first is a pre-notification stage, in which the company makes the announcement and presents a reorganisation draft to the Company Register. In the second stage, the announcement must be published in the Latvian Official

Gazette about the reorganisation project of a company through the acquisition by another one.

In the first stage, the acquiring company announces the reorganisation. Neither the declaration of intent nor the accompanying reorganisation project draft must be made using standardised or binding templates. A state tax of EUR 18 is charged for each company involved, while the cost of publishing the declaration of intent in the Official Gazette amounts to a one-off fee of EUR 9.25.

The board can subsequently call a shareholder's meeting, which however cannot take place sooner than one month after the publication in the Official Gazette. At the meeting, shareholders formally decide whether to reorganise. In the case of a positive deliberation, it must be published in the same Official Gazette. Three months after that second publication, both the acquiring and the acquired companies must officially report the decision to reorganise to the Enterprise Registry. The three-month period allows for shareholders or third parties that object to the reorganisation to express their concerns and contest the decision.

The documents that have to be submitted in this second stage of the process are the application to reorganise, the decision to reorganise, the agreement on reorganisation and the final financial review of the company that was acquired.

The cost of the reorganisation consists of a state tax of EUR 30 to be paid by each company involved and a fee of EUR 9.25 for the publication of the final reorganisation process in the Official Gazette.

The Enterprise Registry evaluates the procedure of acquisition and provides a response within three working days. The various activities required to complete the procedure are presented in Table 4.3.

Table 4.3. Activities, time required and associated fees to reorganise companies through merger by acquisition[1]

Activities	Time and costs associated
1. Preparation of a reorganisation draft for the Enterprise Registry	30 minutes
2. Visit the Enterprise Registry to deliver the reorganisation draft and make the payments	60 minutes + EUR 10 (transport) + 30 minutes (at the Registry) + EUR 45.25
3. Publication in the Official Gazette and waiting time for one month	30 days
4. Meeting to decide on reorganisation and publication in the Official Gazette	60 min + EUR 17
5. After three months, preparation of all documents to be presented in the Enterprise Registry	3 months + 60 minutes
6. Visit the Enterprise Registry, submit documents and make the payments:	60 minutes + EUR 10 (transport) + 30 minutes (at the Enterprise Registry) + EUR 69.25 (fees)
6.1. Application on reorganisation	-
6.2. Decision to reorganise	-
6.3. Agreement on reorganisation	-
6.4. Final financial review of the company that was acquired	-
7. Delivery of positive notification by the Enterprise Registry	72 hours

1. For the purpose of this measurement, it was assumed that the reorganisation is made internally (no payment to any law firm to help through the process), there is a normal amount of creditors (which does not impose any difficulty in making the financial statements of the merging companies and do the closure of accounts) and a lawyer and an accountant are at hand within the companies to follow up the process. It is also assumed that the procedure is conducted in person, not electronically with the use of e-signatures.
Source: Author.

Results without opportunity costs

The sheer administrative cost borne by businesses when they reorganise two companies through the acquisition of one by the other is EUR 1 726.76. Since 342 mergers of this type took place in 2016 in Latvia, the total administrative costs for businesses carrying out this procedure amounted to EUR 590 533.31 in that year. The total time required to complete the process is almost 24 days. In addition, there is also the waiting time of more than four months between some of the administrative activities that have to be conducted (Figure 4.3).

Figure 4.3. Administrative activities and costs of reorganising companies through merger by acquisition (without opportunity costs)

In EUR and as % of the total cost

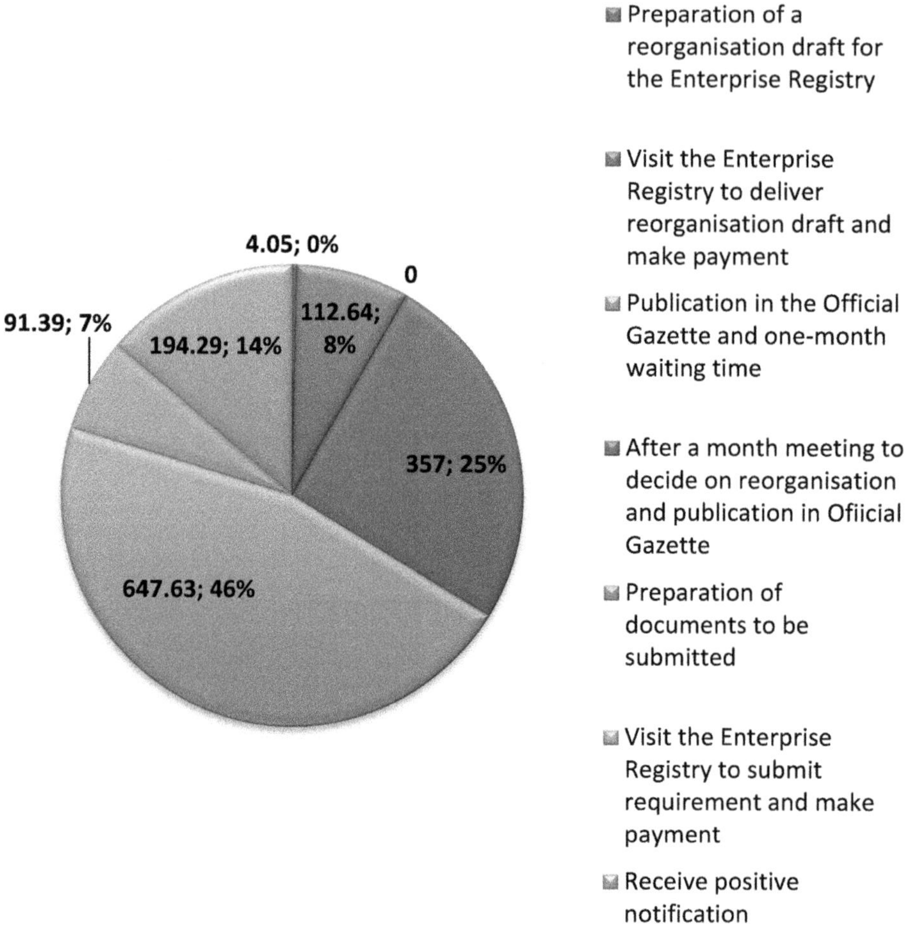

Source: Author.

The main sources of costs are associated with the preparation of the set of documents that has to be delivered to the Enterprise Registry: initial preparation of the draft reorganisation plan (14% of administrative costs), after a month, the preparation of the final agreement on reorganisation (25% of the administrative costs), which should inform creditors about the merger so they can prepare their claims, if any, and after another three months, the final preparation of all documents that have to be presented to the Enterprise Registry (46% of the administrative costs). According to businesses, documents do not change drastically from the initial intention to merge, as this decision is made at the beginning of the process, so the various steps are seen as repetitive by most businesses.

Results with opportunity costs

In this procedure, there are two instances where the companies are affected by significant "waiting time" – the initial one month related to the pre-notification stage and the subsequent three months, during which the companies cannot complete the merging and hence cannot operate as a new entity, until final positive notification from the Enterprise Registry. The assumption here is that the waiting time creates a significant delay in the set-up of a new company, which will not be able to operate as such until a positive decision is granted by the Enterprise Registry.

If the opportunity costs arising from the process were included in the measurement, the administrative cost borne by businesses when they reorganise two companies through acquisition of one by the other would amount to EUR 6 228.31, since it takes more than four months of waiting time to complete the procedure (considered as an opportunity cost). In 2016, 342 mergers of this type took place in Latvia, which brings the overall administrative costs for businesses carrying out this procedure to a total of EUR 2 130 080.63. The overall time to complete the process is 144 days. Figure 4.4 shows the costs and activities of the whole process.

Figure 4.4. Administrative activities and costs reorganising companies through merger by acquisition (including opportunity costs)

In EUR and as % of the total cost

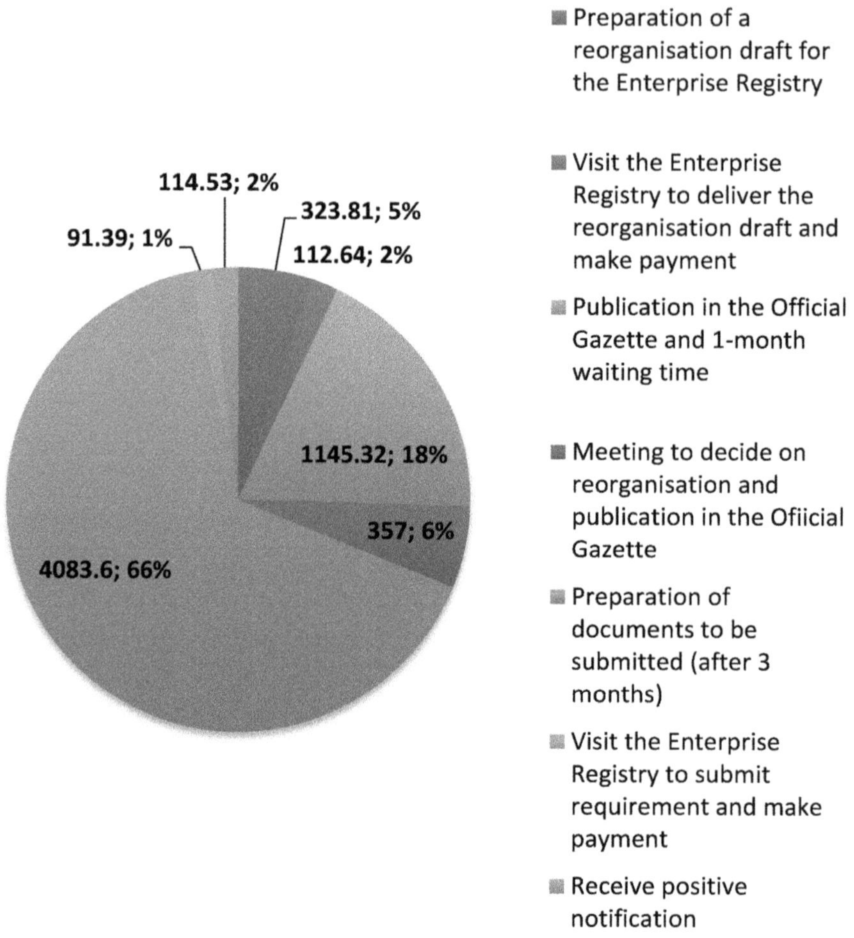

Source: Author.

In this process, 75.39% of the administrative cost is associated with the waiting time that businesses have to spend in order to meet deadlines and get answers from the Enterprise Registry. In this case, that waiting time was calculated as an opportunity cost, since the companies cannot merge until the whole procedure is completed, missing commercial and economic opportunities as a single company. Waiting for an initial month to prepare the reorganisation and then for additional three months to formally submit the reorganisation request to the Enterprise Registry amounts to EUR 4 695.83.

Results of quantification: Possible costs savings for businesses

The three selected procedures mapped and measured by the OECD are relatively straightforward and have already undergone substantial simplification over the years. This notwithstanding, a number of possible costs savings can be identified through the application of the Standard Cost Model (SCM), making these processes less burdensome for businesses. These areas of further improvement can be summarised as follows:

- In terms of the actual registration and licensing to operate granted to both an individual merchant and an LLC with a decreased capital, the process is long and costly. What the OECD mapped and measured above only covers the registration procedure managed by the Enterprise Registry, which is but the initial check of the company's name and legal address. Obtaining a positive notification from the Registry does not lead directly to an authorisation to the applicant to start trading. The latter must comply with further administrative steps, which might trigger quite significant delays, particularly in case VAT fiscal regimes need to be opened and specific licenses are required. The costs associated with this initial procedure amount to the equivalent of EUR 369 for an individual merchant and EUR 478.49 for an LLC with a decreased capital. Considering that further, additional requirements and procedures are foreseen before being authorised to actually start operating, these amounts may be substantial.
- In light of this, the time required for the initial part of the registration procedure appears considerable – slightly more than four and five days (depending on the type of business), from the moment the business starts looking for information on how to apply to when it receives positive notification. Only waiting for three days for a final positive notification is equivalent to EUR 194.29, and the business cannot start operating. Reducing that amount of time might help decrease the administrative costs related to the registration. This would imply having shared databases among registries in order to make the checks performed by the Enterprise Registry quicker.
- Several stakeholders interviewed by the OECD referred to the fact that information is still not very clear on the Enterprise Registry website. Enhancing communication and further facilitating the use of guidelines, templates and examples on the type of information that the Registry requires and checks can have a positive impact on the administrative cost of the procedures, since it would reduce the cases in which applicants feel the need to visit the Registry in person to get clarifications. The administrative costs to businesses could also be cut by reducing the time devoted to becoming familiarised with the procedure (estimated at three hours and equivalent to EUR 24.30) and by streamlining the type of information that has to be presented to the Enterprise Registry.
- The lack of generalised use of e-signatures implies that most applicants visit the Enterprise Registry and they make an appointment with a state notary in order to have their signatures notarised. This means an associated cost to both registration activities, which account for around 25% of the total administrative cost of each procedure. Broader use of e-signatures and the online system could have a positive impact on reducing the cost of the procedure for businesses. For instance, the Enterprise Registry offers a discount of 10% on the state tax charged for the submission of documents to those applicants that use the online system. Combined with the elimination of the EUR 4 fee charged to the applicant for

paying at the Registry, as well as with the elimination of the notarisation requirement thanks to the e-signature certification and of the need to visit the Registry in person, this would reduce the administrative cost for an individual merchant registering on line to EUR 278.47, compared to EUR 369 (or 24.64% less) in the case he/she decides to register at the Enterprise Registry. The administrative cost related to the online registration of an LLC with a decreased capital would be EUR 391.66, instead of EUR 478.49 (or 18.15% less) in the case of an in-person registration.

- With regard to the merger by acquisition procedure, mandating two stages for the process appears to be cumbersome and it increases the administrative costs for businesses. The first pre-notification stage, in which the companies have to prepare a reorganisation draft and present it to the Enterprise Registry could be eliminated, since the companies have made an initial decision to merge and the publication of such intention occurs as a part of the subsequent stage anyway. That would reduce more than one month of waiting time and several payments related to state taxes and publications in the Official Gazette. If the opportunity costs are considered, the elimination of the pre-notification stage would generate savings in the order of EUR 1 581.78 (or 24.40% – i.e. cutting from EUR 6 228.31 to EUR 4 653.46) per business. Including flexibility on the three months for creditors' claims would reduce even more the administrative cost of the procedure, since not all companies require such an amount of time for this activity.

Annex A. Methodology

Methodology for measurement

The Standard Cost Model

The measurement conducted by the OECD and presented in this report (see Chapter 3) refers to costs borne by entrepreneurs and businesses in Latvia when complying with requirements and obligations that are contained in legal instruments, such as the Commercial Law. In particular, the purpose of the quantification exercise was to measure exclusively the administrative burdens imposed on businesses by the selected formalities mentioned above. Accordingly, the measurement does not provide evidence of other types of compliance costs borne by private entities, nor of the costs that affect the public authorities involved in the formalities.[1]

The measurement is largely based on the Standard Cost Model (SCM), a cost assessment methodology originally developed in the Netherlands and which is widely used in several OECD countries since the late 1990s.[2] Annex Box A.1. presents the main concepts and elements of the SCM. Several countries have made adaptations to the methodology, mainly reflecting the specific domestic policy drivers underlying the cost measurements. For the purpose of this exercise, the OECD maintained the main features and parameters of the classical SCM approach, adapting them to the Latvian conditions and previous experiences with such measurements.

Box A A.1. Key concepts and components of the Standard Cost Model

According to the International Standard Cost Model (SCM) Manual, the method is a way of breaking down a regulation into a range of manageable components that can be measured. The SCM does not focus on the policy objectives of each regulation. As such, the measurement focuses only on the administrative steps that must be undertaken in order to comply with regulation and not whether the regulation itself is reasonable or not.

The basic unit of measurement is an information obligation (IO). IOs are the requirements arising from regulation to provide information and data to the public authorities or third parties. IOs can only be completed if some specific administrative activities are undertaken by the economic operator. The SCM estimates the costs of completing each activity. The SCM basic formula is the following:

Cost per administrative activity = Price x Time x Quantity (population x frequency)

The rationale underlying the SCM is represented in the following figure:

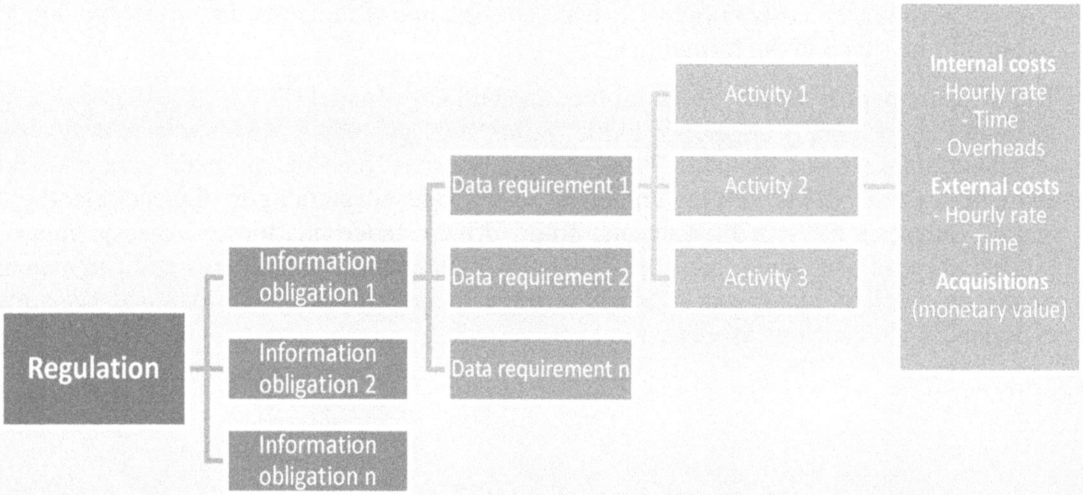

Source: Adapted from SCM Network (2005), International Standard Cost Model Manual, The Hague.

Methodological approach and data sources

The OECD proceeded to a tiered approach to the identification and measurement of the administrative costs associated with the three selected formalities:

- In close collaboration with the Latvian Enterprise Registry, the OECD thoroughly reviewed the relevant laws, implementing regulations and administrative acts regulating the procedures, and conducted a comprehensive mapping of what businesses have to comply with.
- The Enterprise Registry also provided detailed information on the various forms that must be filled in by businesses and administrative fees associated with each procedural step. An integral part of the mapping exercise was also the

identification of all checks that the Registry carries out once the businesses submit their application and information dossiers, as well as the conditions under which the Registry grants a positive response or a request for amendment.

The SCM is a methodology that relies heavily on first-hand information provided by the users of the formalities. To that end, the OECD subsequently tested the "theoretical" information obtained from the mapping exercise through direct interviews with businesses. The interviews took place on site and over the phone or Skype, when entrepreneurs or their representatives visited the Enterprise Registry to complete the paperwork. Interviews were also undertaken with law firms that help businesses go through the procedures.

Assumptions and limitations

The cost calculation process rests on a few assumptions. In particular, the OECD relied on the formulas and standard values that the Latvian institutions are expected to use when performing such measurements. Typically, this occurs during the process of elaborating a regulatory impact analysis (RIA).

Provisions regulating the *ex ante* impact assessment system and methodological guidance are set out in the related Cabinet Instruction of 2009.[3] The Instruction stipulates how the measurement of administrative costs should be made. By administrative costs are meant costs that result from information obligation or storing duties provisions. They should be obtained using the following formula: C = (f x l) x (n x b), where:

- C = Information provision/storing costs
- F = Financial resources required (costs per hour of work)
- I = Time to prepare information
- N = Number of people subject to duty
- B = Frequency per year

The costs per hour of work (F) were estimated using the information gathered by the Central Statistical Bureau of Latvia, in relation to the hourly labour costs of administrative and support service activities in 2016.[4] In the framework of the OECD measurement exercise, the costs per hour of business to handle administrative activities was set at EUR 8.10 per hour.

The number of businesses subject to the three procedures analysed was obtained by official data from the Enterprise Registry. Table A A.1 outlines the distribution of cases in more detail. For the purpose of the measurement, only the positive decisions were taken into consideration.[5]

Table A A.1. Businesses subject to the selected procedures in 2016

Procedure	Decisions together	Positive decision (Registration granted)	Negative decisions (Postponed or refused registration)
Registration of individual merchant	833	603	230
Registration of limited liability company (LLC) with a decreased capital	16 218	10 316	5 902
Mergers between limited liability companies	432	342	90

Source: Latvia -Enterprise Registry.

A number of issues in which caution should be exercised regarding this measurement exercise include:

- While the selected procedures have their legal bases in the Commercial Law, over the years the Enterprise Registry progressively streamlined each of them in order to ease doing business and encourage entrepreneurship. Simplification measures have affected various procedural dimensions, such as the number of interactions and direct visits to the Registry; the compilation of forms and preparatory documents to be presented; the availability of state notaries directly at the Enterprise Registry to notarise signatures, etc. As a result, the requirements established in the law do not necessarily reflect the practice. This discrepancy is not directly explicit in the calculations, which measure the actual costs borne by the businesses. Possible future measures for legal simplification should take this caveat into account when considering the evidence from this measurement exercise.
- The Enterprise Registry offers the possibility to accelerate the procedure, in particular for the registration process, with additional payment. This "fast-track" registration was not taken into consideration for the measurement, as it is not considered common practice, but rather an exception to the normal procedure.
- On the basis of the discussions and interviews held by the OECD, it appears that in most cases applications for registering a company (both an individual merchant and an LLC with decreased capital) refer to legal addresses, for which the agreement of the owner is required. As a consequence, the calculations made by the OECD included the specific step of seeking and including the written consent in the application dossier.
- It was also assumed that documents were presented in Latvian, since this is what the Register requires. If a document is issued in a foreign language, applicants must provide a translation certified by a notary. The additional time and costs that such an operation implies were not considered in the cost measurement.
- A further assumption refers to the notarisation process. Applicants have the option to have recourse to a sworn notary for the recognition of signatures, or directly to a state notary at the Enterprise Registry. Since most of the applicants interviewed by the OECD indicated that they opted for the state notary procedure (see above), the measurement of the costs refers to this latter scenario. For the calculations, the assumption was that the time to get the appointment with the state notary was 24 hours and the cost per notarised signature was EUR 9, which is cheaper than doing it outside the institution.

The data collection for the calculations comes from direct interviews. Since it was not possible to organise focus groups for this purpose, the methodology relied on structured interviews with people familiar with the process (either businesses themselves or law firms providing support to businesses). Three entrepreneurs were interviewed for the procedure involving the registration of an individual merchant, nine for the registration of an LLC with decreased capital and ten lawyers shared their views while doing the merger by acquisition of two companies.

It shall also be noted that the OECD considered measuring opportunity costs linked to the procedure, notably in the case of the reorganisation of companies through merger by acquisition. Including opportunity costs highlights the potential impact of the waiting time. The opportunity cost measures the foregone benefits due to the impossibility to operate the desired economic activity. It was calculated through the rate of return and investments opportunities in the country.

The classical SCM methodology does not foresee the inclusion of opportunity costs for the waiting time. It only focuses on the time dedicated to the administrative activities required to comply with the information obligations. In case a given procedure generates delays or when no clear deadlines exist, waiting time may become a substantial source of costs, rendering the calculation of opportunity costs significant. In the particular case of the Latvian procedure for reorganisation through merger by acquisition, businesses continue operating during the time they need to wait (Stages 1 and 2 of the procedure). However, since the merger cannot take place in practice, businesses might miss possibilities to operate under the reorganised statutes (this might prevent them from expanding their economic activity or force them to postpone decisions that might have brought a benefit to the companies). The OECD measurement therefore provides results from the quantification of cost both with and without opportunity costs in relation to the reorganisation procedure.

Notes

[1] For insights on the cost typology, see OECD (2014), OECD Regulatory Compliance Cost Assessment Guidance, OECD Publishing, Paris, http://dx.doi.org/10.1787/9789264209657-en.

[2] See OECD (2010), Why is Administrative Simplification So Complicated? Looking Beyond 2010, OECD Publishing, Paris, http://dx.doi.org/10.1787/9789264089754-en.

[3] See the Cabinet Instruction No 19 on “Rules for Completing the Initial Impact Assessment of a Draft Legal Act” of 15 December 2009.

[4] Hourly labour costs are total quarterly (annual) labour costs divided by the number of actually worked hours of all employees within a quarter (year).

[5] As a result, the actual costs borne by businesses undergoing the three selected procedures might be higher than those outlined in this report, since negative decisions also generate costs in terms of delays or duplicated procedures.

Annex B. Reducing founding and operation costs and facilitating modern forms of business and finance in Latvia

Reducing founding and operation costs

Mandatory minimum share capital requirements reconsidered

Mandatory share capital requirements for private and public companies have an influence on the level of entrepreneurial activity. The higher the capital figure required for founders to raise when commencing business in the form of a limited liability company, the less entrepreneurial activity is to be expected. While a mandatory share capital was quite common in the 20th century in many European company laws, recent times saw many countries giving up a mandatory capital figure for private companies and lower it for public companies. Mandatory minimum capital requirements lost ground, because such a figure is arbitrary and would be either too high or too low in the large majority of cases. Where the figure is too high, it stifles business and increases the costs of founding one. Where the figure is too low, it does not have a relevant regulatory effect for creditors. In addition, research showed that offering limited liability with lower capital requirements increases the number of enterprises founded. In line with these developments in regulatory practice and science, most stakeholders interviewed in the OECD missions felt that a mandatory minimum share capital for private companies in Latvia is not necessary. In addition, the suggestion was made to reduce the capital figure for public companies.

Latvian law currently requires a minimum amount of equity capital of EUR 2 800 for private limited liability companies (Section 185 of the Commercial Law). Under specific circumstances, the equity capital can be lower than this figure (described in Section 186 of the Commercial Law). In essence, such a company may have a maximum of five members, all of them need to be natural persons, the directors may only be persons who are members of the company at the same time and each member is only associated with one such type of company. For public companies, the minimum capital figure is set at EUR 35 000 (Section 225 of the Commercial Law).

For the reasons named above, Latvia might be interested in analysing the approaches of other jurisdictions that have abolished the minimum share capital requirement entirely for private companies. In English company law, for example, private limited companies can be founded without a minimum share capital requirement. European law does not require any minimum figure for private companies as the relevant directive rules only apply to public companies. Article 45 of Directive 2017/1132 requires a minimum share capital of EUR 25 000 only for public companies in Latvia. Hence, the relevant figure in Section 225 of the Commercial Law could be reduced from EUR 35 000 to EUR 25 000. While the current English Companies Act 2006 requires a minimum share capital of GBP 50 000, only 25% – i.e. GBP 12 500 – have to be paid up (Sections 586, 761, 763 of the Companies Act 2006).

Model articles by ministerial order

Model articles for private and public companies offer a reduction of the costs of founding a company, while at the same time maintaining legal certainty. As a result, entrepreneurs can have access to companies as an organisational form for businesses without the need for costly advice on their articles. English law has used this approach for many decades and other OECD jurisdictions, such as Germany, have followed this best practice. In essence, English law offers model articles for founders of private and public companies. These model articles are established by ministerial order and reflect the standard articles that the majority of founders would choose. Model articles are based on a ministerial order instead of statutory law to provide an easy mechanism to adapt them to changing business needs. An act of parliament is not required; rather the relevant company law empowers the minister accordingly. Further, a section in the company law provides that the model articles apply unless they are not excluded or amended by the members of the company. This makes the model articles automatic, but optional. Founders and shareholders can opt out and amend them, if they prefer different rules. However, if founders do not amend them, they get a reliable standard set of articles for free.

Box A B.1. Model articles under English law

Section 20 of the English Companies Act 2006 reads as follows:

"Default application of model articles:

(1) On the formation of a limited company;

(a) if articles are not registered, or

(b) if articles are registered, in so far as they do not exclude or modify the relevant model articles.

The relevant model articles (as far as applicable) form part of the company's articles in the same manner and to the same extent as if articles in the form of those articles had been duly registered.

(2) The "relevant model articles" means the model articles prescribed for a company of that description as in force at the date on which the company is registered."

For more information on model articles under English law, see www.gov.uk/guidance/model-articles-of-association- for-limited-companies.

Latvian law currently does not provide for such a combined mechanism in the Commercial Law and by way of ministerial order. The Enterprise Registry seems to offer standard articles on its website. However, they neither have the effect of a ministerial order, nor are they equipped with automatic application by a section in the Commercial Law. In particular, small and medium-sized enterprises (SMEs) are potential beneficiaries of model articles that apply automatically by force of law if not excluded or amended. Model articles based on a default provision in the Commercial Law would have the advantage of clear legal status. Such articles may, in particular, fill gaps where SMEs do not have or are not willing to spend the relevant funds for tailored legal advice.

Modern management structures and responsibilities

Latvian public companies are currently required to have a two-tier board structure, i.e. a board of directors and a supervisory council. Private companies need to have a board of directors, but have the choice whether to establish a supervisory council or not. Consideration might be given to the request of some stakeholders to allow for choice between one-tier and two-tier board structures. In a one tier-board, the board of directors has the power to both manage and supervise the management of the company. Usually, executive directors exert the management function while non-executive directors supervise management. In the two-tier board-structure currently prescribed in Latvia, the board is charged with managing the business and the supervisory council controls the board. Allowing choice between the one-tier and the two-tier board structure could provide businesses with the opportunity to select the corporate governance model that fits their needs. Both models could be designed in a robust way to ensure the desired level of management supervision. The option to choose between one- and two-tier board structures is already part of Latvian law for the Societas Europaea. Many European member states offer a choice between one- and two-tier boards, for instance in France, Italy, Lithuania and the Netherlands.

A further area for consideration is the optimal level of loyalty, care and risk taking by directors of private and public companies in Latvia. Currently, Section 169 of the Commercial Law provides only a short description of the loyalty and care required from directors. The law refers to the "duties of an honest and careful manager" and leaves it to the courts to develop further details by way of interpretation. The stakeholder interviews revealed some indication that the reference to the "honest and careful manager" might create both over- and under-regulation at the same time. The provision might over-regulate by preventing desired risk taking and under-regulate by failing to capture wrongdoers. It might make sense to discuss whether moving to a model that combines directors' duties regulated in more detail with a business judgement rule that encourages desired risk taking. Regulatory examples include English law for the more detailed regulation of directors' duties. For more than a decade, directors' duties are laid down in a higher level of detail in Sections 170 and following in the English Companies Act 2006. German law introduced a business judgement rule in § 93 of the German Law for Public Companies (*Aktiengesetz)* following the US-American model. In essence, a director is not liable under the business judgement rule if he or she took a business decision adequately well-informed and in good faith in the interests of the company.

Closely connected to the duties of directors is the enforcement of liability if such duties are breached. When considering whether boards show the optimal level of care, loyalty and risk taking, enforcement mechanisms such as Section 172 of the Commercial Law might be considered together with substantive law rules. If the result is that the enforcement of director liability is wanting, the introduction of wider powers of minority shareholders to bring claims on behalf of the company might be an option. The introduction of the power for shareholders to bring derivate claims under certain conditions in the English Companies Act 2006, Sections 260 to 264, is generally considered successful. A core element of the English model is the introduction of a procedural vetting process in which the court filters whether an action has potential merit and may continue or whether it seems wrongly constructed and should not further burden the company.

Section 173 of the Latvian Commercial Law allows the shareholders to release members of the board of directors or the supervisory council from liability for breaches of duties.

In its current wording, this rule seems to provide the shareholders with the power to release from liability even in those cases in which the company cannot satisfy all creditors' claims. This might create incentives for shareholders to ratify breaches – possibly by themselves in their function as director – when companies are in financial distress to the detriment of creditors. If this is considered as unhelpful practice, inserting a limiting wording into Section 173 preventing such ratifications might be a way forward.

Broadening the view to private sector activities, helpful facts may be revealed by an observation of the market for directors and officers insurance (D&O insurance). Stakeholders indicated that D&O insurance is not very common in Latvia, but is slowly emerging. Further, stakeholders reported that D&O insurance products are offered by European and international insurers rather than by local insurance companies. At least two things might require attention. First, it might be helpful to find out why the local insurance market is not offering D&O insurance or why local products are not competitively priced. Second, if D&O insurance products become more prevalent, attention should be given to whether or not they are undermining the *ex ante* behavioural effects of directors' duties. If directors are not worried any longer, whether they might be held liable for breaches because they are insured, then directors' duties might lose their disciplinary effect. Other jurisdictions have reacted to such a development by limiting the company's contribution to the costs of D&O insurance and by setting minimum liability figures that cannot be insured. Moving ahead, Latvia may consider various options in this regard, taking into account a number of factors and how they may best be adapted to the particular circumstances in Latvia. Amongst these factors are the deterrence effect of liability on the willingness to be a director, the amount of remuneration directors receive and how effectively reputational concerns may already serve as an incentive for directors to take their duties seriously.

A sophisticated framework for mergers and divisions

All stakeholders spoke with one voice when evaluating the rules applying to mergers, divisions and restructurings. The common evaluation is that these rules provide a basic framework, but are in need of improvement. Stakeholders made the following suggestions to either introduce possibilities or clarify the existing rules to reduce uncertainty:

- introduce rules on spin-off restructurings
- simplify the reorganisation of a private company as a public company
- simplify the merger of two subsidiary companies
- introduce a straightforward possibility to transfer a local branch to another local company
- clarify the exact point in time when a reconstruction becomes effective
- reconsider whether the announcement of registering a merger is necessary as the stakeholders are informed anyway
- simplify the rules on informing creditors about a merger
- simplify share conversions
- facilitate squeeze-outs for private and non-listed public companies.

Reforming the law of mergers and divisions needs to take account of the requirements of Title II of Directive 2017/1132 on mergers and divisions of limited liability companies.

This would require a decision on whether the mandatory EU requirements for public companies shall also apply to private companies. Generally, it seems to be preferred practice to reduce the administrative burden for private companies as far as shareholder and creditor interests allow. In other words, split rules for public and private companies are used to avoid over-regulation of private companies. Similarly, many EU member countries make intensive use of the options and possibilities provided by the directive to reduce the administrative burden for mergers and divisions involving public companies.

Formal coherence

Several stakeholders mentioned unease concerning the inconsistent registration of shares in public companies and indicated that thought should be given to including private companies by way of optional share registration. Currently registration of share ownership is not mandatory for all joint stock companies. A number of stakeholders felt that this often can provide a way for some shareholders in public companies to hide (for the wrong purposes). The depository registration is currently only optional. The necessity to set up a register for the beneficial ownership of shares should be considered for reform in this area of the law. In particular, it provides an opportunity to harmonise registration requirements regarding public companies.

If shares in a private company are registered, then the transfer of such shares could be freed from having public notaries involved, which would further reduce costs. In a less radical approach, this would, however, only be an optional registration. If the register was not used, the prime responsibility would remain with the company. Some stakeholders went even further and argued that private companies should have their shares mandatorily registered with a central entity because the boards were not always efficient in managing the share register.

Facilitating modern forms of business and finance

A modern corporate finance law as the backbone of innovative finance

As the European Union's Capital Market Union Action Plan[1] puts forward, deeper and integrated capital markets promise to provide businesses with a greater choice of funding at lower cost and offer new investment opportunities for investors. Law has an important role to play in expanding investment choice and in minimising the cost of finance. This concerns both equity and debt finance. The role of the law in corporate finance is two-fold. First, it can enable financial arrangements that parties would have trouble creating based only on freedom of contract. An example is the provision of different classes of shares by company law. Second, it can contribute to reducing the cost of business finance. An example is finding the right balance between creditor protection and flexibility for shareholders in capital restructurings. If creditors are prone to expropriation, the cost of debt finance will rise. At the same time, overly limiting shareholder flexibility will make equity finance more costly. The latter shows that legal reform should keep in mind that market actors will react to the corporate finance framework they find. If the law does not create the optimal balance, equity and/or debt investors will charge a premium for the finance provided. As a consequence, fewer projects and businesses would be financed. Hence, the ultimate goal should be to minimise the average cost of both equity and debt finance.

The stakeholder interviews in Latvia revealed a general consensus that updating core provisions of classic corporate finance law would be beneficial to support business finance. Providing investors and managers with finance options and clarity of law would put them in a position to develop innovative solutions. Hence, the starting point for an innovative finance practice can be high-quality core provisions of business finance law. In this regard, the Latvian Commercial Law already provides a stable basis. Stakeholders suggested to further broaden the range of finance options available and provide businesses with more certainty.

A minor, but potential helpful change called for by stakeholders is to allow the nominal value of shares to be determined in cents. Currently, Section 186(1) of the Latvian Commercial Law requires the nominal value of equity capital of a private company to be expressed in whole euros. Consequently, a nominal value of one cent or ten cents is prohibited for private companies. The nominal value of a share in a public company may not be less than ten cents according to Section 230(2) of the Latvian Commercial Law. These restrictions for private and public companies may complicate certain forms of sophisticated business participation. Lower amounts may become necessary after incorporation, for example to implement the introduction of new classes of shares or capital restructurings. Allowing one-cent shares for both private and public companies in Latvia - as a possibility - could increase the flexibility for businesses to arrange their finance structure, as there seems to be low risk this would lead to costs or further problems in legal reality.

A further basic feature of shares that might be discussed is the introduction of no par value shares, i.e. shares without a nominal value. The shares of both private and public companies are required to have a fixed nominal (or par) value, according to Section 186(1) of the Latvian Commercial Law. There is a trend in many countries to move away from a mandatory nominal value of shares as they are often associated with complications in share capital adjustments and could lead to confusion for market participants. Countries that allow no par value shares are, for example, Australia, Germany, Portugal and South Africa. While non par value shares may be attractive for businesses and their investors, they require careful drafting when reforming the law. One of the options to consider for Latvia is to offer businesses a choice between nominal (par) and no par value shares. This is the approach that the German *Aktiengesetz* currently takes.

Another possibility asked for by stakeholders is to facilitate the creation of classes of shares in private companies. The Latvian Commercial Law recognises the possibility of creating different classes of shares in Section 227. This provision, however, is to be found in the rules for public companies. As a result, the question arose whether different classes of shares can be created for private companies. While the Latvian Commercial Law does not contain a prohibition to create different share classes in private companies, the uncertainty regarding class rights created by the current law is often reported to create problems for private companies. Similar to some OECD countries (e.g., Germany, United States and the United Kingdom), Latvia may encourage the freedom for businesses and their equity investors to create different classes of shares, with different classes allowing the possibility to offer different equity participation to different types of investors. As there are different types of investors with different types of investment interests and profiles in the market, more flexibility in terms of share classes may encourage more equity investment at lower cost. The rise of start-up finance and private equity finance in the United States and the United Kingdom was – among other things – based on the ability of their legal systems to provide different share classes in private companies.

The logic that class rights are a means to satisfy the investment interests of different types of equity investors with the expectation that this will lead to more equity finance offered at lower cost may also call for a reconsideration of the regulation of class rights for public companies. The rules on class rights in Section 227 of the Latvian Commercial Law currently seem to limit the type of class rights that can be created. This section only mentions different rights with respect to: 1) receiving dividends; 2) receiving a liquidation quota; and 3) voting rights at a meeting of stockholders. Consequently, it seems that all other types of class rights are not recognised by Latvian law. However, investors and companies may have good reasons to provide certain shares with other types of administrative, financial or information rights. The occasion of looking into the issue of class rights for private companies might be combined with reconsidering a more liberal approach to the definition of classes of shares. One solution might be to do away with the enumeration of different types of class rights and instead only define what constitutes a class of shares. It would then be left to the businesses and their investors to negotiate the types of class rights that fit their needs. This approach is currently taken both by English and German company law.

Similar considerations concern the regulation of preference shares. Preference shares are regulated in Sections 231 to 234 of the Latvian Commercial Law. Further provisions concern the position of preference shareholders, in particular in reorganisation. First, the fact that Sections 231 and following of the Latvian Commercial Law only apply to public companies raised the concern of several stakeholders that preference shares might be considered unavailable to private companies. At the least, even if registers and courts accept preference shares in private companies, their position is fraught with uncertainty, which increases the cost of capital. Second, a number of stakeholders suggested deregulating the rules on preference shares. Section 232(1) of the Latvian Commercial Law leaves it to the articles of association to determine the rights of preference shares. However, stakeholders felt that the following subsections limit the freedom to create preference shares that fit their needs. In particular, subsection (3) determines that preferences with special dividend rights acquire voting rights only if dividends are not paid for two successive accounting years. It was suggested to consider deregulation of the law on preference shares and generally allow the shareholders to determine the rights associated with preference shares. In addition, stakeholders felt that there is scope to simplify the currently drawn-out procedure for voiding preference shares.

A further related issue is the facilitation of employee share schemes. The Latvian Commercial Law provides rules on employee shares only for public companies in Section 255. Stakeholders have expressed that this creates uncertainty on whether employee shares can be used in private companies. Employee shares can play a useful role for private companies, in particular to provide equity-based incentives. Going beyond the reduced applicability of Section 255 of the Latvian Commercial Law, thought might be given to equipping employee shares in general with further benefits. English law, for example, provides the following benefits for employee share schemes: 1) as a default position, directors do not require specific authority to allot employee shares; 2) pre-emption rights do not apply to employee shares; 3) a public company is not prevented from giving financial assistance for the acquisition of shares for an employee share scheme; 4) the rules on share buy-backs are less strict for employee shares. As a related side note, stakeholders also suggested the general relaxation of the rules on share buy-backs.

Moving on to exit options, it might be worthwhile discussing the costs and benefits of the right of first refusal in Section 189 of the Latvian Commercial Law. This area of law has been the focus of recent reform. According to section 189 of the Latvian Commercial Law, the other shareholders have a right of first refusal if a shareholder in a private company sells his or her shares. While such a rule can found in some cases, it might reduce the attraction of being a shareholder in a private company. The obligation to offer shares to the other shareholders after entering into a purchase agreement may create uncertainty for the original share purchase agreements and make the sale of shares in a private company a lengthy process. As a result, shareholders interested in exiting private companies will find it more difficult to find a buyer willing to incur the costs for a share purchase that might not happen in the end. This in turn may add further difficulties to the already reduced exit options regarding private companies. If investors know that exit is difficult, they might refrain from investing in the first place. Therefore, equity finance for private companies can become more costly and scarce. In English and German law a right of first refusal does not exist as a default position in private company law. The shareholders are always free to negotiate such a right for their company and establish it in the articles of association. Latvia might benefit from monitoring how the practice as regards the right of first refusal develops over time and consider adjustments, if this seems beneficial.

A final brief point concerns tax law although it is generally not within the ambit of this report. It might be interesting to note, though, that stakeholders asked to reconsider the point in time at which profit accrues in terms of tax law for share options. Choosing the point in time when they are exercised rather than when they are issued might make them more attractive in practice.

Supporting recent trends in business finance

Stakeholders reported a recent initiative in the FinTech market driven by remarkable consensus. This is encouraging as it offers opportunities for fruitful discussions on how law can support FinTech and other initiatives related to blockchains and initial coin offerings (ICO). One issue particularly emphasised in the stakeholder interviews was crowdfunding. From the point of view of the legislature, crowdfunding is particularly challenging. It is a relatively new phenomenon and it sits somewhat uneasily between issues of consumer law and capital markets law. Internationally, different approaches to regulating crowdfunding can be discerned. While crowdfunding is considered as possibly offering a useful source of finance and deserving support, careful consideration should be given to ensure that consumers are not lured into deceptive investments. There is certainly no one-size-fits-all approach to regulating crowdfunding and the particularities of the Latvian capital market need to be respected.

In this regard, consideration might be given to facilitating share pledges. Some shareholders thought it might be helpful to offer a solution for those cases, where a large number of share pledges needs to be registered.

A balanced capital markets law initiative

A number of stakeholders called for a better connection between the Commercial Law (including the company law elements) and the Financial Instruments Law. Stakeholders feel that the Commercial Law is not always written with public finance markets in mind, which might also be explained by the history and development of the Commercial Law. While it could be a major undertaking, it may be worthwhile, though, and could support the development of deeper capital markets in Latvia. In addition, it could be tied into the European Union's Capital Market Union Action Plan initiative and thus gain further momentum. Such a regulatory analysis and initiative may, however, not lose sight of small companies and their needs. Innovative solutions can be found to develop a more integrated approach to company and capital markets law while at the same time maintaining a focus on small and medium-sized companies and their regulatory interests.

Share registration

A further issue for consideration might be the registration of shares. Stakeholders mentioned three issues with regard to reordering the law on shareholder registration. First, there seems to be a need to achieve a consistent framework for the registration of shares in public companies. Currently, not all shareholders of public companies are listed. Second, the registration of beneficial owners of shares can be considered in the interest of fraud avoidance. Third, there appears to be a need for discussion on whether an (optional) registration shall be offered for shareholders in private companies. The background to these issues are reports from some stakeholders that directors sometimes make registration mistakes or even collude with certain shareholders. In the past, this led to, for example, 145% shareholders' presence in a general meeting. Similarly, in the past there were illegal takeovers of companies using manipulations of shareholders' lists. Furthermore, stakeholders reported problems of finding shareholders, which had negative consequences for company reorganisations, as their involvement was required.

The issue of extending shareholder registration may raise the following two issues: 1) which institution is best suited to manage the registration process; 2) which institution is the point of contact for outsiders who want to obtain information on registered shares. For the particular situation of Latvia, two possible institutions were mentioned by shareholders to manage registrations: the Enterprise Registry or the Central Depository. Here, choice requires a balancing act considering existing competences and structures and the future benefits of economies of scale through the centralisation of registration competences. In any case, however, the information on share ownership should be available from one central entity for outsiders requiring information. External data fragmentation should be avoided in the interest of providing a one-stop data provision institution.

Note

1 See https://ec.europa.eu/info/business-economy-euro/growth-and-investment/capital-markets-union_en.

ORGANISATION FOR ECONOMIC CO-OPERATION AND DEVELOPMENT

The OECD is a unique forum where governments work together to address the economic, social and environmental challenges of globalisation. The OECD is also at the forefront of efforts to understand and to help governments respond to new developments and concerns, such as corporate governance, the information economy and the challenges of an ageing population. The Organisation provides a setting where governments can compare policy experiences, seek answers to common problems, identify good practice and work to co-ordinate domestic and international policies.

The OECD member countries are: Australia, Austria, Belgium, Canada, Chile, Colombia, the Czech Republic, Denmark, Estonia, Finland, France, Germany, Greece, Hungary, Iceland, Ireland, Israel, Italy, Japan, Korea, Latvia, Lithuania, Luxembourg, Mexico, the Netherlands, New Zealand, Norway, Poland, Portugal, the Slovak Republic, Slovenia, Spain, Sweden, Switzerland, Turkey, the United Kingdom and the United States. The European Union takes part in the work of the OECD.

OECD Publishing disseminates widely the results of the Organisation's statistics gathering and research on economic, social and environmental issues, as well as the conventions, guidelines and standards agreed by its members.

OECD PUBLISHING, 2, rue André-Pascal, 75775 PARIS CEDEX 16
(42 2018 33 1 P) ISBN 978-92-64-30340-9 – 2018

www.ingramcontent.com/pod-product-compliance
Ingram Content Group UK Ltd.
Pitfield, Milton Keynes, MK11 3LW, UK
UKHW051503290926
15471UKWH00008B/1392

9 789264 303409